The JehuFactor

What's Next for America

*Releasing a new generation into their inheritance
to be all God wants them to be and do all God wants them to do*

By Larry E. Dozier, M.Ed.

Publishing   your   "Master   Pieces"

Copyright © 2015 by Larry E. Dozier

All rights reserved. No part of this publication may be reproduced, distributed, or transmitted in any form or by any means, including photocopying, recording, or other electronic or mechanical methods, without the prior written permission of the publisher, except in the case of brief quotations embodied in critical reviews and certain other noncommercial uses permitted by copyright law. For permission requests, write to the author, addressed "Attention Larry Dozier: Permissions" at larrynjc@yahoo.com

Special discounts are available on quantity purchases by corporations, associations, and others. For details on orders by US trade bookstores and wholesalers, contact the author at the email address above.

Unless otherwise noted Scripture quotations are from THE HOLY BIBLE, NEW INTERNATIONAL VERSION®, NIV® Copyright © 1973, 1978, 1984, 2011 by Biblica, Inc.® Used by permission. All rights reserved worldwide.
Scripture quotations taken from the Amplified® Bible,
Copyright © 1954, 1958, 1962, 1964, 1965, 1987 by The Lockman Foundation
Used by permission." (www.Lockman.org)
Scripture quotations are from The Holy Bible, English Standard Version® (ESV®), copyright © 2001 by Crossway, a publishing ministry of Good News Publishers.
Used by permission. All rights reserved.
Scripture is taken from GOD'S WORD®, © 1995 God's Word to the Nations. Used by permission of Baker Publishing Group.
Scripture taken from the NEW AMERICAN STANDARD BIBLE®, Copyright © 1960, 1962, 1963, 1968, 1971, 1972, 1973, 1975, 1977, 1995 by The Lockman Foundation. Used by permission.

The New Testament in Modern English

Verses from the Complete Jewish Bible by David H. Stern. Copyright © 1998. All rights reserved. Used by permission of Messianic Jewish Publishers, 6120 Day Long Lane, Clarksville, MD 21029. www.messianicjewish.net.

Scripture quotations marked "KJV" are taken from the Holy Bible, King James Version, Cambridge, 1769.

Scripture quotations from THE MESSAGE. Copyright © by Eugene H. Peterson 1993, 1994, 1995, 1996, 2000, 2001, 2002. Used by permission of Tyndale House Publishers, Inc.

Scripture quotations marked (TLB) are taken from The Living Bible copyright © 1971. Used by permission of Tyndale House Publishers, Inc., Carol Stream, Illinois 60188. All rights reserved.

Scripture quotations marked HCSB are taken from the Holman Christian Standard Bible®, Used by Permission HCSB ©1999,2000,2002,2003,2009 Holman Bible Publishers. Holman Christian Standard Bible®, Holman CSB®, and HCSB® are federally registered trademarks of Holman Bible Publishers.

Editor: Spirit-Led Publishing

Cover Designer: Spirit-Led Publishing

Photo of Larry Dozier: Sharon Jepsen

First Edition, 2015

ISBN: 978-1943011230

Publisher: Spirit-Led Publishing

Dedication

I dedicate this book to all those that have shaped my life, especially during my early days as a young Christian:

To my mom and dad, Billy and Valle Dozier, for teaching me the ways of God.

To my Youth Pastor, Curtis French, for teaching and mentoring me to know God through worship.

To Cecil and Helen Bartel for teaching me the Bible and answering all of my questions.

And Evangelist Barry Wood for leading me to Christ through his preaching.

One of my favorite Bible verses is:

I can do *all things* through Christ who strengthens me.
Phillipians 4:13

Acknowledgements

Special thanks to Dr. Charles Robinson, CEO of Spirit-Led Publishing, whose tireless guidance, encouragement, and refining made this book all that God has desired it to be.

Special thanks to my talented friend for over 40 years, Eloise Elaine Ernst Schneider, Christian artist, https://fineartamerica.com/profiles/eloise-elaine-schneider.html. Without her encouragement, skills and talents, this book would not have been the same.

Endorsement

In a time of uncertainty and fear, Larry has presented a Biblical compilation that will certainly give some sense to the historical timeline we face today. There have been many predictions as to what will happen next in the world only to find they don't come to pass. With skepticism on the rise you will find Larry Dozier making application to the seriousness of our day using Biblical Truths to explain what we must be prepared for. With the political landscape becoming more confusing by the day, you will find this book not only relevant but filled with encouragement for the future. He emphasizes that when families practice a biblical lifestyle that even our enemies will be at peace with us.

What's next for America is not only for the scholar, but anyone who is a serious pursuer for solutions for America. You will be informed through Larry's research and challenged by his own personal story to arrive at these principles. You will be better informed for the future as to not fall into the trap of fear that so many are purveying, but instead, be able to know how to prepare for what you are seeing.

Kerry Kirkwood

Kerry is the founding pastor of Trinity Fellowship in Tyler, Texas, founded in 1987. He was Larry Dozier's pastor for three years, and he is the author of *The Power of Imagination, The Power of Blessing,* and *The Power of Right Thinking.*

Foreword

A new generation of prophetic authors is arising. Larry Dozier is among that group. *The Jehu Factor, What's Next for America* represents a "now" word not only for America but the nations of the world. For as America goes, so go the nations.

Combining practical application to the times of Elijah and Elisha with a keen sense of the times we are now living in, Larry seamlessly develops a strong argument on where he sees the nation heading. Additionally, Larry helps each of us overcome the roadblocks to our spiritual growth, both internal and external.

The Apostle Peter admonished us to "Gird yourselves up in the spirit of your minds." I Peter 1:13. You are about to embark on a journey into the very heart of Jehu, the future King of Israel who single-handedly took down the most hated, feared, and revered character of the Bible – Queen Jezebel. The principality that empowered Jezebel and who bears her name still exists. *She* is everywhere... in Hollywood, in the Feminist Movement, in the fashion industry, and in the *church*.

I highly recommend this book as required reading for those who want to overcome the spirit of this age and to help usher in the next phase of the Kingdom of God. To be forewarned is to be forearmed.

December 30th, 2016

Dr. Charles Robinson

Author of the "Let Heaven Invade the Seven Mountains" and the "Becoming Melchizedek" book series.

In this book, you will learn…

1. What's next on America's prophetic time clock.
2. Where America is found in Bible prophecy.
3. The ancient Hebrew secret to knowing God.
4. The Biblical meaning and significance of delegated authority.
5. What Donald Trump and Jehu have in common.
6. How to activate the Elisha Double Anointing in your life.
7. How to implement the "Jesus Model of Discipleship".
8. A current prophetic view of American politics.
9. The parallels of ancient Israel and modern America.
10. The State of American Public Education.
11. A God-inspired Strategy to restore America back to God.

Table of Contents

Chapter 1: The God Factor 10

Chapter 2: A Tale of Two Countries 43

Chapter 3: The Legacy of a Prophet... 80

Chapter 4: Double for Your Trouble 8976

Chapter 5: The Jesus Model of Discipleship................................. 122

Chapter 6: God's Word, Will and Ways... 160

Chapter 7: What's Next for America?.. 197

Bibliography 243

About the Author 244

Chapter 1: The God Factor

About four years ago, the Lord sent me to live with my mom on our family farm in Athens, Texas. This move followed the untimely death of my younger brother who lived with my mom. I rented my home, sold or gave away everything except some clothes. After arriving at our farm, the Lord showed me that he wanted me to start spending much more time with him in prayer, Bible study, meditation, and worship. Jesus called this, 'sitting at his feet,' in Luke 10: 38-42. He also introduced me to a new daily discipline. He said, "Sit in your favorite chair, empty your mind of your agenda, and then ask me, 'What is on your heart today, Father?' Then, just sit and listen."

As a result, the Lord has given me four major revelations that are protocols/prerequisites for the Body of Christ to implement in overcoming the Spirit of Ahab and Jezebel stronghold in America. Elijah, Elisha, the school of prophets and Jehu understood these four truths while honoring the supporting protocols. The bottom line is that as we learn to accept God's rules in the following four areas, we begin to have a dramatic influence on our circumstances and those that will receive from us. I will share more about all of these later in this book. But for now, here's the list.

1. Understanding God's Delegated Authority
2. Activating the Ancient Model of Discipleship
3. Restoring the Jewish Roots of Christianity
4. Receiving the Elisha Double Anointing

Like the Book of Ecclesiastes says, there's a time to talk and a time to listen. And for me, this was a time to listen. I remembered Psalm 46:10, *"Be still, and know that I am God: I will be exalted among the heathen, I will be exalted in the earth."* We used to sing a rendition of those words in my church choir. After looking up the Hebrew word translated as "be still and know," I began to see that God wanted me to cease from my efforts to perform and only rest in his presence (like John 15 teaches) while listening to his still small voice like Elijah did. I also realized that I was in the presence of the one that knows all; and I was doing all the talking!

As a result, I began to understand and activate the "God Factor" in my life. That enabled me to experience a deeper resting and abiding in the Spirit of God like in John 15, while actively listening to/for his voice to speak to me. As long as I was talking, I could only hear my voice, and I couldn't hear his. An elementary school teacher once told me, "Larry, you have two ears and one mouth. That means you're supposed to listen at least twice as much as you talk." It was excellent advice, don't you think?

I had no idea how much of a challenge that would be. At first, I had to deal with all kinds of competing thoughts; so I had to learn to quiet my spirit and shut my mouth. Then I began to discover how God used that time to speak "sweet somethings" in my spiritual ears. Also, God began to revolutionize my prayer life - especially my intercessory prayer for the healing of America.

Eventually and progressively, the Lord gave me four prophetic teachings - three of which I published on my online e-column entitled, *"Bible Influences on America,"* at www.christianpost.com, a Salem Media Communications Company. These articles quickly became my most popular articles. Then, the Lord began to share more and more with me, using the foundational principles of my articles. This book is a compilation of what I have learned.

You're probably thinking, "The God Factor! What does that mean?" Well, that's what I'll attempt to explain in this chapter, using various examples from my personal experiences.

First, I want to share with you about the God Factor protocols in my life experiences, while defining what it means to me and its relationship to "The Jehu Factor." And what it could mean to you. I've noticed the God Factor can overcome any negative influences in my life. Like the Law of Aerodynamics overcomes the Law of Gravity, those who honor the God Factor Protocols will discover how to overcome life's negative influences and soar over them like an eagle.

The God Factor Defined

Here's a simple nonreligious definition of the God Factor. The God Factor is an invisible force with specific protocols that will cause things like the Law of Gravity and the Law of Sowing and Reaping always to work. I'll share more about that later in this chapter. But for now, just remember there are specific protocols that are required for us to approach our invisible-spiritual King just like there are rules to contact a judge in a visible, tangible court of law in America. Honoring those protocols will empower us to successfully navigate through the challenges of life while enabling The God Factor to work on our behalf. For example, 2 Chronicles 7:14 says, *"If my people who are called by my name will humble themselves, pray, seek my face and turn from their wicked ways, I will hear their prayers, forgive their sin and heal their land."*

In 2 Chronicles 7:14, the God Factor protocol is presented in four steps:

1. Humble yourselves
2. Pray
3. Seek my face
4. Turn from your wicked ways.

The benefits are that God says he'll:
- <u>Hear</u> our prayers
- <u>Forgive</u> our sins
- <u>Heal</u> our land.

Every time we locate the word "If" in the Bible as a heavenly protocol, there are similar benefits or rewards for honoring the specific rules. I call this The God Factor. And it's as sure to happen as gravity if we will comply with the proper protocols!

One such protocol is

The Principle of Delegated Authority

God created the heavens, earth, man, and woman while providing everything Adam and Eve needed. And according to Genesis 1, God delegated the authority to rule over the earth to Adam and Eve. Adam was given the power to name all of the animals, subdue the earth, be fruitful and take dominion over everything on the ground. Then God gave them "happiness" boundaries for living on the land. In other words, if they didn't follow the pleasure limits, they would experience the unhappy consequences of their disobedience. Pretty clear and straightforward really - don't you think?

In Genesis 1: 26-38, God delegated the overseeing of the earth to Adam and Eve.

Then God said, "Let Us make man in Our image, according to Our likeness; let them have dominion over the fish of the sea, over the birds of the air, and over the cattle, over all the earth and over every creeping thing that creeps on the earth." So God created man in His image; in the image of God He created him; male and female He created them. Then God blessed them, and God said to them, "<u>Be fruitful</u> and <u>multiply</u>; fill the earth and subdue it; <u>have dominion</u> over the fish of the sea, *over the birds of the air, and <u>over every living thing</u> that moves on the earth."*

As you have seen, Genesis 1 clearly documents the delegated authority being transferred from Creator-God to Adam and Eve. Then after the Serpent - the Devil - tempted Adam and Eve, causing them to eat the forbidden fruit, the Devil usurped Adam and Eve's God-given authority, stealing it for his purposes. As a result, Adam and Eve brought upon themselves a curse, rather than enjoying the blessings that their Creator God had given to them. God told them not to eat of the tree of the knowledge of good and evil. And if they did, they would surely die. The Hebrew word that was translated "die" more literally meant "to be separated from." God was warning them that if they ate of the tree of the knowledge of good and evil, it would cause them to be separated from his glory.

Everyone Reaps What They Sow!

The immediate consequence of Adam's sin was that he would have to work by the sweat of his brow for his provision. But the immediate impact of Eve's sin was that she would have to suffer pain in childbirth and be under man's authority. However, the third consequence of their sin was the passing down of their iniquity to their two sons – Cain and Abel. As a result, Cain eventually murdered his brother, Able, because of his covetousness and disobedience. Adam and Eve were guilty of the same basic sins, but their disobedience led to their "deaths," while Cain was guilty of killing his brother. It was the same sin with different circumstances, but Adam and Eve's sin ended in death as did Cain's – spiritually and physically. (See the story of Cain and Abel in Genesis 4.)

> **Wisdom Key:**
> **What parents allow in moderation, their children will excuse in excess.**

According to the Genesis story, it matters what one generation does (sows) because the next generation will inherit (reap) from their actions. And Genesis 8:22 affirms that all children will obtain from their parents according to what their parents sowed, whether blessings or curses.

The LORD is longsuffering, and of great mercy, forgiving iniquity and transgression, and by no means clearing the guilty, visiting the iniquity of the fathers upon the children unto the third and fourth generation. (Numbers 14:18)

The longsuffering of God is the God Factor at work because God spoke the writing of the following words to Noah after the flood. It's commonly called "The Law of Sowing and Reaping."

"While the earth remains, Seedtime and harvest, Cold and heat, winter and summer, And day and night Shall not cease." (Genesis 8:22)

Jeremiah 1:12 (AMP) says, "Then said the Lord to me, You have seen well, for I am alert and active, watching over My word to perform it."

That is why Galatians 6:7-8 warns,

"Do not be deceived, God is not mocked; for whatever a man sows, that he will also reap. For he who sows to his flesh will of the flesh reap corruption, but he who sows to the Spirit will of the Spirit reap everlasting life."

Through these and other scriptures, I have been learning how essential it is for me to get into agreement with God's written and revealed word, while confessing it over myself, my family, my church, my friends and those at my job.

Of course, others that might see the goodness of God in my life may call it 'The Larry Factor' because I was the one that God used. But I knew it was the God Factor working in and through me. That is what Jesus (Yeshua/Yashua in the Hebrew) provided on the cross - *wholeness*. He took back what the Devil had stolen and returned it to man, the decedents of Adam and Eve – you and I. And the authority to take dominion over the earth was passed down to all humanity through Noah, Abraham, Isaac and Jacob, King David and eventually, Jesus, who restored it all for anyone that will believe. But as Jesus taught to the twelve Apostles, it's our responsibility to learn how to pray effectively, "Thy will be done on earth (the visible realm) as it is heaven" (the invisible dimension).

The Romanization of Christianity

When the Roman Emperor Constantine decided to make Christianity the state religion in Rome, he systematically got rid of honoring the Feasts, the Sabbath, the Hebrew calendar and anything else that he considered "Jewish." He re-made Christianity in his image. I discovered that I have been guilty of the same thing. One day I thought, "Why do I honor all of the Ten Commandments except the Sabbath?" In my search for truth, I heard a Bible teacher say "...because the Sabbath was part of Judaism, not Christianity, we don't honor the Sabbath."

First, that is not accurate. For the first 300 years of Christianity, all Christians honored the Sabbath and the Feasts. Further, no human or religion should decide this commandment is in and that one is out, referring to the Ten Commandments. God has not given anyone the authority to pick and choose which of his words they want to follow. And no scripture tells the followers of Jesus to stop honoring the Sabbath or the Feasts. I suggest to you that Constantine started this tragic error and the Protestants in the 1500's continued it, while we have blindly received and believed the same after all of these years. That is what the devil did. He said to Adam and Eve, "Surely God hath not said."

God Honors Authority – Satan Usurps It

Jesus was Jewish and honored all of the Jewish Holy Days. Jesus is also our bride; so, do we say that we don't need to honor marriage anymore because it's Jewish? The whole purpose of the Sabbath was to teach the Hebrews and Jews that God is their source and to learn how to rest. God, the Father (Yahweh) is the one that makes them prosper. And they don't need to work day and night or seven days a week to "make ends meet." Their great God will provide for them. God wanted them to remember that he is their Creator, their God and Heavenly Father who passionately wants the best for them. But for us to be successful today, we need to learn how to follow the Manufacturer's Manual – The Bible.

Every time my life doesn't run properly, I go back to the Manufacturer's Manual to find out how to repair it. We also need to discover how and how often to get a tune up, when to change our spark plugs and get an oil change (a new Holy Spirit infilling.) The Feasts' benefits are in the Bible – The Owner's Manual.

To that point, during the time of Emperor Constantine (AD 285 – AD 337) the Jews were systematically cut off from Christianity, thus starting the Rome Empire version of Christianity. Although Constantine ended Christian persecution in the Roman Empire, as I have said, he also removed the Feasts, the Sabbath and the Hebrew calendar. And to this day, many believe anti-Semitism still exists but it is much more subtle. Some scholars believe that it appears in various modern Christian doctrines as the refusal to honor the Feasts, the Hebrew calendar, and the Sabbath. These which were not "Jewish," but were 'God's feasts' and more accurately translated as "special appointments with Yahweh (God the Father)," refer to a date more easily identified in the Hebrew calendar, when gifts were exchanged. The more accurate Hebrew Calendar is based on the moon cycles, while Americans use the Gregorian calendar that is based on the solar cycles.

Perhaps you will remember when God spoke to Moses as recorded in the book of Exodus and told him what to do and what to say to Pharaoh of Egypt? And every single time God honored the words of Moses to Pharaoh, he worked an incredible miracle to convince Pharaoh to let the Hebrew slaves go free. That was the God Factor being manifested – not just once but ten times! It appeared every time God spoke to Moses and told him to speak to Pharaoh to quit enslaving the Israelites and let them go free. And when the Israelites started to cross the Red Sea, the Bible says that God put a wall of fire between the Israelites and the Egyptian army, giving the Israelites enough time to cross the Red Sea without being slaughtered by the Egyptian army. That's what I'm calling The God Factor. However, it does not have to be a prolific miracle. And because God has chosen to partner with humankind (his creation) to collaborate with him to release his goodness and glory on earth, I also refer to the God Factor as The Noah Factor, referring to the flood; and the Moses Factor, referring to the miraculous things God did through him. The Joshua Factor identifies Joshua as the one God used to supernaturally lead the Israelites to take the land that was promised to them by God. Of course, there are many other examples of the God Factor in the Bible. God partners with me and any other willing person to express his goodness and glory to his creation on earth. What excellent access to God we have!

The God Factor can also be an occurrence that has no natural or rational explanation. Many people call this phenomenon "luck or serendipity." But when considering Biblical wisdom, there is no such thing as luck. It has been said, "Success is when preparation meets opportunity." Similarly, "luck" is when someone purposefully or inadvertently cooperates with God's laws/principles, as found in the Bible, regardless of their religious persuasion. For example, the Law of Gravity will cause any object dropped from a ten-foot tall ladder to fall whether one agrees with it or believes in it or not. The Law of Gravity is an equal opportunity employer. It doesn't care what color a person is, what religion he/she is or anything else. If a person wisely cooperates with gravity, that person will enjoy the related success. To overcome the Law of Gravity, scientists have learned to work with a higher law, the Law of Aerodynamics, which enables them to fly their jet planes, overcoming the Law of Gravity.

Suffice it to say for now that individual God Factor keys have frequently empowered me to overcome the negative influences of lust and sickness. Of course, people called it 'The Larry Factor', but I knew better. I knew I was nothing without God.

The God Factor in My Life Story

As a young child, my mom took me to a small Baptist church in Grand Prairie, Texas. She required me to attend Sunday school to learn about God and the Bible, and to meet new like-minded friends of my age. After Sunday school, we would attend their worship service as I watched my mom sing like a bird in the church choir with her beautiful soprano voice and contagious smile. Occasionally she would sing a solo. They called that "the special music." That made sense to me. I thought my mother was unique, and I loved to hear her make music in her heart to God with the songs she sang – in and out of church services. When my family went on long trips to visit relatives, my mom and I would start singing songs to pass the time. The whole family joined in the singing. We had a great time!

My mother taught me how to sing too. At the age of ten, I was already singing religious and nonreligious solos. However, I learned to sing a specific song called, "On Top of Old Smokey" for my dad. It was his favorite song. Sometimes I would sing by myself and other times my mother would sing it, or she and I would sing it as a duet – all because my dad loved that song. But later, I sang in the choir at my local elementary school and learned a lot of new songs - religious and secular. I remember when my elementary public school choir teacher asked me if I sang with a vibrato naturally. I told her that it was just the way it usually comes out of my mouth. I know now that I learned how to sing with a vibrato by singing along with my mom. And as a 10-year-old boy, all of that practice began to pay off. I was one of the children chosen to sing in a professional presentation of *"The King and I"* musical. I even got to sing a short solo in it! As a result, I was later offered a spot in the Texas Boys Choir; however, my dad didn't want me to join The Texas Boys' Choir. He wanted me to pursue athletics. So, that is what I did.

When I was 12, I played on a little league baseball team where I led the league in home runs, batting average, and RBI's while being awarded the MVP trophy. What an amazing summer that was! I also competed in the local newspaper's essay competition by writing about my baseball coach and submitting it to the paper for judging. I earned a free round-trip all expenses paid vacation trip to Hot Springs Arkansas for my family and my coach. We had a fabulous time!

The next summer, I played baseball and led the city league in home runs again. I was on top of the world! The following season, we won the state baseball tournament championship. I was enjoying outstanding success until something unthinkable happened. I dislocated my right elbow playing in my high school spring football practice. My arm was never the same again.

Although I could still hit the ball very well, I didn't have the same strength and accuracy to throw the ball. As a result, I began to move away from baseball toward football.

As a growing teenager, I began to experience inner conflicts about what I thought the truth was. If there was a God and Savior named Jesus, why were there so many different denominations, I thought? My dad was raised a Baptist and mom a Methodist, but after they got married, my mom joined the Baptist church. Their differences served to motivate me to search for what truth was and what it was not, rather than just accept the teachings from a denomination or person without allowing God to confirm it to me.

I loved the church music, the people, and my parents; but I had not learned to love their God and follow Jesus like the Bible teaches. As a result, I began to read a lot about the different kinds of religions and listen to various preachers like Billy Graham, who later had a great influence on my life.

My Personal Testimony

In my early teen years, I had a "best friend" that I met in junior high school while playing football. That friendship later proved to be a divine appointment and my friend turned out to be an outstanding athlete. I won't say his name because I didn't get his permission. At 17 years of age, while attending a Falls Creek Church Camp in Oklahoma with my church youth group, I accepted Jesus Christ as my personal savior.

And that changed everything! It was my friend's family and his church youth director that created an environment that led me to Christ, taught me the Bible, and treated me as if I was one of their children until I graduated from high school. We were also encouraged to pray with the high school football team thanks to our Christian coaches. We learned to freely and enthusiastically share our faith in Christ at school and on the football field. Such today is more difficult, but not impossible.

Those who trained me stayed in touch with me through my freshman year as I played football at the University of Texas in Austin under the late-great Coach Darrell Royal. For the first time, I began to experience The God Factor in my life – the God Factor being loosely defined as what happens when a believer in Christ learns to know God and make him known in such a way that circumstances and people around him/her are dramatically changed for the better. I have had the honor of experiencing how The God Factor can change anything or everything concerning my circumstances, personal life, and relationships. That's one reason why I am writing this book. I want to help you experience the God Factor in your life by standing on my shoulders of revelation and understanding to walk on the troubled waters of life.

Throughout the entire Bible, people's lives, their circumstances and relationships have been completely transformed and suddenly changed as the result of faith in God and obedience to his teachings and special instructions. Moses, Abraham, King David and Joshua are a few great examples.

My friend, whatever is pulling you down now, there's a higher law called the Law of Spirit and Life (see Romans 8) that can enable you to fly on the wings of a great eagle to overcome the law of sin and death and rise above your circumstances. The Law of Spirit and Life will enable you to overcome the Law of Sin and Death like the Law Aerodynamics overcomes the Law of Gravity.

Please don't sit back and say, "That's impossible." That is what people used to say about flying airplanes until someone discovered the Law of Aerodynamics. I have found that The Law of Spirit and Life can overcome The Law of Sin and Death if we will only identify, understand, and activate its mystical power and authority as it is found in Romans 8:2.

"For the law of the Spirit of life in Christ Jesus has made me free from the law of sin and death."
(Romans 8: 2, NKJV)

While in high school, thanks to God, my parents, and my high school coaches, I became one of the highest recruited high school football players in the country. I received over 250 letters from various university football programs from all over the USA wanting me to visit their schools to consider playing football for them. They offered me a full 4-year scholarship to play football, saying they would pay for everything! What a life, I thought. But after one successful year at UT, I realized that my heart and desires were moving more and more toward God and away from football, as Jesus began to take first place in my heart and affections. And for the first time in my life, sports didn't have the preeminence.

I believed that I had found the truth I had been looking for as a child - in Jesus. After an undefeated season playing football at UT, I made an appointment with the late Coach Darrell Royal to resign from the football team. Coach Royal was very kind, generous and gracious. I thought he was a great coach, but an even greater Christian man. However, I believed I already had The Greatest Coach and Teacher of all time recruiting me to be on his team - the Son of God, Jesus Christ, who invited me to follow him. And by following him, I would learn how to be a team player and a team leader, while learning to excel in the most important game of all – the Game of Life. Wow! What a great opportunity! I was very excited.

The Return of the God Factor!

Following my resignation from the UT Longhorn Football Team, I was awarded a full-tuition music scholarship at Midwestern University in Wichita Falls, Texas, where I attended for the next two years. During that time, I also had a part-time job as the Music and Youth Director at a Baptist church in Wichita Falls, Texas. As I applied what I had learned from those that mentored me in my hometown of Grand Prairie, I began to see another move of God in the young people in Wichita Falls, like what had happened in Grand Prairie.

Once I was playing basketball with some guys I didn't know. And suddenly I heard a still small voice say to me, "That guy has acute asthma. If you pray for him, I'll heal him." So I asked him if he had severe asthma. He said, "Yes, why?" And I said God told me that if I can pray for you, he'll heal you. He gave me permission to pray for him and he stated that he was instantly healed. That was later confirmed by his doctor. Similar healing miracles happened throughout the 1970's and continue to this day.

The most recent healing miracle was with my mom. While she and I were sitting, and enjoying watching TV, she told me that she suddenly couldn't use the entire right side of her body. She tried to use her right hand and arm, but there was no response to her efforts. Then suddenly, I felt the Spirit of God jump inside of me, motivating me to pray for her like in the Bible. So, I commanded the entire right side of her body to be healed and for the blood clot to melt. Immediately after prayer, she started using her whole right side with no problems! I was reminded of John 7: 38: **"He that believeth on me, as the**

scripture hath said, out of his belly shall flow rivers of living water."

About three days later, I felt led to take her to the doctor. The doctor immediately sent her to the hospital only to find out that she had no health problems that were caused by a stroke or heart attack, although an MRI confirmed that she had experienced a stroke. Over the past three years, God has also healed her of Diabetes Type 2, Chronic Sinusitis, and Dementia fully validated by various medical doctors!

> **Wisdom Key:**
> **Sometimes when you feel the only thing you have left is God,**
> **You realize he's all that you really need.**

As I mentioned earlier, I accepted a part-time Music and Youth Director position at a small Baptist Church in Wichita Falls while I was attending Midwestern University. That meant the Lord provided me a part-time job and a full tuition scholarship. Life was good! During that time, we began experiencing the miraculous power of God (The God Factor) in our small Baptist church youth group in Wichita Falls, Texas. We wanted to allow God to move in our lives like he did in the New Testament. Our church youth group grew from about ten regular members to over 80 active young people in just about seven months! In that same year, we had our annual church-wide revival service that broke all attendance records. And according to those that had been at the church for many years, the revival meeting was unprecedented.

What was going on there? I had no clue. I just simply tried to let my light shine and prayed that my words would be salt and light to its hearers while leading some to faith in Christ. Eager young people just kept joining us. There were such large numbers exemplified by a great hungering and thirsting for God that we began to have special youth meetings every night in our small chapel that was located in our local church. What an amazing experience! We met for three straight weeks every night in the church chapel until parents and church leaders started complaining. After that, contention began to cause division in our church and youth group. And within just a few weeks, that incredible move of God that had lit a fire in our hearts was snuffed out by a tsunami of criticism and complaints. That opposition caused a powerful move of God to leave about as quickly as it had begun. Unfortunately, I was too young and immature to deal effectively with that kind of a problem.

I believe that kind of story has been repeated for many years in many religious institutions (AKA: Churches) across America. That is one big reason why the next big move of God will be mostly in the marketplace. God will be in control of the next spiritual renewal, and no religion will be able to direct it or snuff it out.

Jesus openly invited us to follow him, not follow a human-made religion. He also gave us clear instructions about how to follow him. He said, *"Deny yourself, Take up your cross daily and follow Me." (Luke 9:23).* What part of those words do we not understand?

A Time of Rapid Change

With three years of college completed, I quit school and began singing full time as a traveling, singing evangelist. Various ministers that I met invited me to be their "singing evangelist" as they called it in the Baptist churches in the 1970's. To this day, I've never found out what happened to that little Baptist church in Wichita Falls, Texas after I left.

Little did I know that the God Factor was about to change everything for me ... again. During this time,

I learned to put my faith in one of my favorite Bible verses, Proverbs 3: 5-6.

"Trust in the Lord with all of your heart and lean not on your own understanding. In all your ways acknowledge Him, And He will direct your paths." (Proverbs 3: 5-6, NKJV)

After one year of traveling and singing, my parents suddenly offered me a proposition. They said if I would quit my singing career and come live with them for a year, they would provide me with free room and board while I completed my bachelor degree. I told them I didn't have the money, so they also agreed to help me get a full-time job to pay for my schooling. The short answer to what happened is that they did what they promised and I did too. In May of 1976, I graduated with a Bachelor of Science, moved out, and got a full-time job, because I was laid-off after about six months from the job they helped me get. But that was all right with me. I was able to graduate from college and get a major job that was in line with my personal interests.

Suddenly, at age 26, I got a phone call from my aunt. She asked me to pray for her because her 15-year-old daughter was missing. By this time, I had a reputation of being a prayer warrior, because I had prayed for some people that were instantly healed of various diseases. Deeply grieved by this news, I decided to pray and fast until I heard from God about my cousin. On the third day, I received a vision (a mental picture), showing me exactly where my cousin was and who was with her. I did not know any of them except for my cousin. While praying, I was suddenly able to see details of where she was as if I was flying over the house like Superman with X-ray vision. I could see inside and outside of the house. It was unbelievable! I had never experienced anything like that before.

So I called my aunt and described in detail what I had seen, although I had no idea where it was, except that it was a small house on an island off the Texas coast. At that time, I didn't even know that Texas had islands off its coastline.

After a brief conversation with my aunt, she knew which friends my cousin was with, what house they were in, and exactly where the house was located. My aunt later told me that she had the number to that house and called it, finding my cousin there! The mystery was solved! Although my family and friends began to call those kinds of things miracles, I knew that they were The God Factor at work.

> **Wisdom Key:**
> **Inquire of the Lord Like David. Since God knows everything and he wants the best for us, we would be wise to ask him for solutions to all of our problems like King David did.**

> **A Wisdom Key:**
> **Our Covenant Blessings**
> **According to the Bible, the Feasts, the Sabbath, etc. were established by our Creator-God showing us how to know him, while activating the many benefits of God's blood covenant with humankind through Jesus Christ. Like Jesus said, "Thy will be done on earth as it is heaven."**

Our benefits are in the invisible realm. It's our job to identify them, believe them, and take them into our lives and circumstances by faith.

Here Are the Benefits
Psalm 103 (KJV)

"Bless the LORD, O my soul: and all that is within me, bless his holy name.

² Bless the LORD, O my soul, and forget not all his benefits:

³ Who forgiveth all thine iniquities; who healeth all thy diseases;

⁴ Who redeemeth thy life from destruction; who crowneth thee with lovingkindness and tender mercies;

⁵ Who satisfieth thy mouth with good things; so that thy youth is renewed like the eagles.

⁶ The LORD executeth righteousness and judgment for all that are oppressed.

⁷ He made known his ways unto Moses, his acts unto the children of Israel.

⁸ The LORD is merciful and gracious, slow to anger, and plenteous in mercy.

⁹ He will not always chide: neither will he keep his anger forever.

¹⁰ He hath not dealt with us after our sins; nor rewarded us according to our iniquities.

¹¹ For as the heaven is high above the earth, so great is his mercy toward them that fear him.

¹² *As far as the east is from the west, so far hath he removed our transgressions from us.*

¹³ *Like as a father pitieth his children, so the* L*ORD* *pitieth them that fear him.*

¹⁴ *For he knoweth our frame; he remembereth that we are dust.*

¹⁵ *As for man, his days are as grass: as a flower of the field, so he flourisheth.*

¹⁶ *For the wind passeth over it, and it is gone; and the place thereof shall know it no more.*

¹⁷ *But the mercy of the* L*ORD* *is from everlasting to everlasting upon them that fear him, and his righteousness unto children's children;*

¹⁸ *To such as keep his covenant and to those that remember his commandments to do them."*

And when we make a mistake, God is faithful and just to forgive and cleanse us, if we'll confess our shortcomings to him (1 John 1: 9).

So when your train gets off its track, stop, look and listen. <u>Stop</u> and confess your sin to God, <u>look</u> to the Bible for your instructions, and <u>listen</u> to what God says to you.

If we will honor the God Factor protocol found in his Word, Will and Ways, we will enjoy the same signs, wonders, miracles, supernatural provision and increase as the early Christians. But when we don't, we won't – in other words, no honor – no benefits. What or who we honor reveals our faith and obedience in that thing or person.

> **Wisdom Key: What you honor will increase.**
>
> **What you dishonor you will decrease.**

Like Jesus said, *According to your faith be it unto you*.

What you believe shapes what you think. What you think shapes what you do. What you do shapes who you are, and who you are shapes how you see things.

How you see things determines your worldview. And your worldview determines your actions. Your actions determine your habits and your habits determine your character.

And it all starts with one thought!

"As a man thinketh in his heart so is he" (Proverbs 23:7). (KJV)

If you have a heart problem, take Romans 12: 1-2 as a one-a-day vitamin:

> *"I beseech you therefore, brethren, by the mercies of God, that you present your bodies a*

living sacrifice, holy, acceptable to God, which is your reasonable service. And do not be conformed to this world, but be transformed by the renewing of your mind, that you may prove what is that good and acceptable and perfect will of God." (KJV)

Chapter 2: A Tale of Two Countries

The United States of America was fundamentally built on Judeo-Christian values and principles that were found in the Old and New Testaments of the Bible. For example, both Christians and Jews have agreed that the Ten Commandments and the teachings of the Old Testament (*The Torah* in Hebrew) were given to humanity by their Creator (Yahweh-God the Father in Hebrew). That is why our American laws, especially in documents like the US Constitution and the Declaration of Independence, have recognized and honored the Ten Commandments as the basis for all American laws.

Even our federal government has a picture of Moses on the front of the US Supreme Court building along with an artistic depiction of the 10 Commandments. As a result, both countries have embraced capitalistic, free enterprise principles when creating their economic systems and supporting governments. As such, the way they view the world and their related ideologies and philosophies are very similar and compatible. Perhaps that is one reason why America and Israel have been strong allies since 1948. That is why, I believe, both countries fundamentally have a Biblical worldview;

thus, these are two nations with one worldview – a Biblical Worldview.

I guess you noticed that I didn't say America was founded on a "Christian Worldview." An honest review of American history will uncover the Jewish roots of Christianity and the critical financial assistance Jewish people provided to George Washington during the American Revolutionary War against Great Britain. The founders of America were more influenced by the teachings of the Bible and the Jews than any other religion, philosophy or ideology of their time. That is why they wrote about "principles" and "truths." And that's why they acknowledged God by calling him "Creator", while declaring that "all men are created equal and endowed by their Creator with certain unalienable rights" in the Declaration of Independence.

That alone is an indictment of American Christians today, revealing how far the American Public Educational System has steered away from the original course of America's founding principles. Today, we have science books that teach our children evolutionary theory as if it's a scientific fact and refuse to include "Intelligent Design". They also claim that teaching God as our creator (Intelligent

Design) is unconstitutional, although our Declaration of Independence clearly affirms that God created man and our US Constitution explicitly states the freedom of Religion for all Americans.

Why has this happened? I believe it has happened because many Christians have been suffering from a severe case of "The Prophet Jonah Syndrome." Perhaps it's best illustrated by the following statement made by British statesman Edmund Burke:

> **"All that is necessary for evil to triumph is for good men to do nothing."**

God has always held his people responsible for the success or failure of their governments. America is no exception. Historically, people's government has always been a reflection of the condition of the people of God. Like Jonah, Americans today have been antagonistic toward the American Public Educational System. And like Jonah, although God has been speaking to his people to go to their local public schools and influence them, most Christians have started their religious K-12 schools, homeschooled their children, or sent their children to their local church academies.

As a result, they have refused to get involved and make needed changes to their local public schools. And like when Jonah was in the storm asleep in the bottom of the ship and the other sailors had to throw him out to calm the sea, God is speaking to American Christians likewise to be thrown out of their religious comfort zones to become salt and light to our American schools. When American Christians take our responsibility before God to be salt and light to our public schools, God will cause the public school leaders and teachers to turn from their wicked ways just like what happened in the ancient city of Nineveh.

Check out what the Declaration of Independence says:

America's Great Religious Document

The Fourth of July is America's birthday. The anniversary of the giving of the Declaration of Independence gives us a good chance to reflect on our nation's religious roots.

The best way to observe our country's birthday is to re-read and re-examine our Declaration of Independence and to rededicate ourselves to the principles of our nation's founding document.

The Declaration of Independence is the official and unequivocal affirmation by the American people of their belief and faith in God. It affirms God's existence as a "self-evident" truth that requires no further discussion or debate. The nation created by the great Declaration is God's country. The right it defines is God-given. The actions of its signers are God-inspired.

The Declaration contains five references to God — God as supreme Lawmaker, God as Creator of all men, God as the Source of all rights, God as the world's supreme Judge, and God as our Protector on whom we can rely.

The Declaration of Independence declares that each of us was created. If we were created, we must have had a Creator. The Declaration of Independence declares that each of us is created equal in the eyes of God. This means equally endowed with unalienable rights. It is not to say that all are born with equal capabilities, as obviously, they are not. Nor does it mean that all of us can be made equal, as Communist dogma alleges. Naturally and realistically, as the modern discovery of DNA now confirms, each of God's creatures is unequal and different in every other way from every other person who has ever lived or ever will live on this earth.

The Declaration of Independence proclaims that life and liberty are the unalienable gifts of God — natural rights — which no person or government can rightfully take away. It affirms that the purpose of government is to secure our God-given unalienable individual rights and that government derives its powers from the consent of the governed, from the

> people. Our Declaration reduced government from master to servant, for the first time in history.
>
> **Knowledge of our Declaration of Independence should be required of all schoolchildren.** The unchangeable Declaration of Independence forever pledges the firm reliance of the American people on the continued protection of God's Divine Providence. Pupils should be taught that many of the men who signed it paid dearly for their courage — and that's why we can enjoy our freedom and independence. © Eagle Forum
>
> <u>Eagle Forum</u> has been leading the pro-family movement since 1972. Its mission is to enable conservative and pro-family men and women to participate in the process of self-government and public policy-making so that America will continue to be a land of individual liberty, respect for life and family integrity, public and private virtue, and private enterprise.

How did America go from honoring God in the Declaration of Independence to dishonoring God through many foolish choices we have made over the past 60 - 80 years?

Let's look at how the same thing happened to the nation of Israel and perhaps that will help us understand the answer to that question.

THEY DID NOT REMEMBER HOW GOOD GOD HAD BEEN (Psalm 106:7).

Americans have a lifestyle that is better than 97% of the world. That is why so many people are trying to immigrate here. We are surrounded by excess food, water, houses, cars, police protection and the right to own guns to protect ourselves.

Of course, not everyone in America has those excesses available to them. But most Americans have at least their basic needs covered if only by their government or local food pantry. However, like ancient Israel from whom we get our Judeo-Christian roots, we have forgotten how good God has been to us.

Are we a grateful nation?

Do we honor God with our time, money, businesses and religions? Do we thank God for our wealth and privileges? According to the New Testament, the people are the church, not a physical building. And we worship a Jewish Messiah who honored the Feasts and the Sabbath as recorded in the New Testament, yet we don't honor the Feasts and the Sabbath because we think they're "Jewish," not Christian.

Jesus, a Jewish carpenter, said, *"Deny yourself, take up your cross and follow me."*

If we follow Jesus, wouldn't that include honoring the Sabbath and the Feasts like he did? I believe this kind of ambiguity in today's Christianity along with other even more severe conditions of the body of Christ must be addressed. I think I have found some pragmatic solutions to these questions and others, which I will share later in this and other chapters in this book.

I believe the same corruption that was experienced in ancient Israel during the reign of King Ahab and Queen Jezebel is happening to America today. I also believe that God has a similar solution for America today that he had for the Israelites in 2 Kings 8-10. But first, we'll take a look at the state of America today and compare it to Israel during the time of Ahab and Jezebel.

What Is the State of America Now?

Our government's response to our 240 years of religious freedom has been to push God out of our schools and to restrict God in our government, the marketplace and our military, creating an explosive increase in home schooling, private schools, and charter schools. And sadly, many American Christians have been embracing a "Prophet Jonah" attitude toward our US Public Schools and Government.

What is the result? The ancient spirit of Jezebel has a foothold in our nation's government. But you can't have a Jezebel without an Ahab. The Prophet Jonah Syndrome evidenced in many Americans has produced similar results as did the rule of King Ahab, enabling the federal government to increase our taxes, ignore illegal immigration, grossly mismanage our tax dollars and manage our country lawlessly, all the while enriching themselves at our expense, creating a double standard. Many politicians have lied to and deceived the American public, using slight-of-hand techniques, calling our attention to one activity to distract us from another.

In short, American Christians have allowed our federal government to enslave us with higher taxes and a corrupt government that steals from the rich, gives to the poor, blames others for their problems and increases the government's power and influence by promising to pay off their constituencies with free government handouts given overtly and covertly. Just as God has given Christians all of the authority and power they need to successfully and righteously rule on earth, they should at the least vote and be involved in the political process.

When Christians don't vote, they're playing the role of King Ahab. They get mad about something and start complaining about it at home. Then they decide to complain to their government representatives. And like Jezebel, their agents take care of it. For example, although you knew their government giveaways were wrong, you justified them by considering how you've been mistreated, creating a victim mindset and an entitlement stronghold in your thinking. After all, you justify, they owe it to me because of what they've done to me or a friend or family member.

Wisdom Key:
If you see yourself as a helpless victim, you'll never rise above the prison of your circumstances.

Benjamin Franklin wisely said, "When the people find they can vote themselves money from the treasury, it will be the end of the republic."

Let's consider a similar communication between Ahab and Jezebel regarding theft.

The 4th of the Ten Commandments states, "Thou shalt not steal." The definition of stealing is when a person or group takes something of value from another without his/her permission.

When the government decides that they can force the sale of another's property because it is in the "highest and best use" of that property, the government is stealing. Besides, the highest and best use of real estate is totally subjective. Perhaps that phrase should be changed to something more objective. Like, *Thou shalt not steal!*

When anyone takes property from another without his/her permission, they are thieves – period. That is what Jezebel did, while Ahab looked the other way, enabling her despicable and corrupt ways. American Christians are guilty of the same thing. Like Ahab, the body of Christ has allowed the Spirit of Jezebel to steal from Americans, giving it a fancy legal name – *"Eminent Domain*." And the US Supreme Court has even affirmed that kind of heavy-handed theft in the name of progress. It's quite evident that attorneys wrote and helped pass real estate laws for their benefit. Guess who determines *the highest and best use* practices of the Eminent Domain laws? Attorneys! Guess who enabled them to implement those laws? Americans!

Is that fair? Why does God hold American Christians responsible for the corrupt condition of America today even if we haven't committed the same sins? First, God created the earth and gave (delegated) full authority to Adam and Eve to be fruitful, take dominion and multiply (Genesis 1-2).

Although Satan stole their power and control from them, Jesus gave it back to all descendants of Adam and Eve who will believe, receive and conceive the new birth of the Kingdom of God. As a benefit of that new birth blood covenant, we have the authority to make earth whatever we want it to be. In Genesis, immediately following the flood, God spoke to Noah and said that he would never again destroy the earth with water. And he stated that as long as the earth remains, so will seedtime and harvest.

Just as a farmer can grow his/her favorite foods in a garden, Christians can cultivate their favorite kind of life, country, and government. In other words, for us to complain about our government is as ridiculous as farmers complaining about the specific food items that they have in their gardens. America has what we've sown and grown. And if we don't like it, then we need to quit blaming everyone else and everything else, take responsibility for it and start a new life of sowing and growing the incorruptible seeds (words) of God into our hearts.

The good news is that we can grow anything in life that we don't have. In short, if you're in need of something, you can learn how to develop it. Clearly communicated in Deuteronomy 28, God was saying to his people that if they wanted to be blessed and to prosper, they should follow his specific teachings, which is sowing good seed for a plentiful harvest of blessings. But, if they wanted to take another course of action (sow different seeds into their lives), they would reap curses. God is saying the same thing to America today.

Deuteronomy 28 (NIV)
Blessings for Obedience:

"If you fully obey the LORD *your God and carefully follow all his commands I give you today, the* LORD *your God will set you high above all the nations on earth. ² All these blessings will come on you and accompany you if you obey the* LORD *your God…. However, if you do not obey the* LORD *your God and do not carefully follow all his commands and decrees I am giving you today, all these curses will come on you and overtake you."*

Galatians says it this way, *"Be not deceived. God is not mocked. Whatsoever a man sows that shall he also reap. If he sows to the flesh, he will of the flesh reap corruption. If he sows to the Spirit, he will of the Spirit reap eternal life." (KJV)*

2 Chronicles 7:14 teaches the same principle of personal responsibility with sowing and reaping.

"If my people who are called by name will humble themselves, pray, seek my face and turn from their wicked way, I will hear their prayers, forgive their sin and heal their land."

It is time for us to **humble ourselves** (confess our sins according to I John 1:9 and be teachable) and to **pray** (petition God to give us his mercy, grace, and wisdom to walk in his word, will and ways).

After doing this, we **seek God's face** (honor God in all of the ways that the Bible teaches). Furthermore, we **turn from our wicked ways** (the Bible calls this "repentance"). Another way to say repent is to stop compromising and sowing to the flesh and start sowing to the Spirit of God.

Parallels of Ancient Israel and America

1. THEY SACRIFICED THEIR SONS AND DAUGHTERS

    In a word: <u>Abortion</u>. (Psalm 106:37-41)

2. THEY BOWED DOWN TO IDOLS AND IMAGES (Psalm 106:19)

Fame and fortune have become more important than God. We now worship the same "bull god" as Israel did. But we call it the "Bull" of the NY Stock Exchange.

3. THEY FORGOT THEIR SAVIOR (Psalm 106:21)

On November 14, 2014, the first Muslim prayer service was held in our National Cathedral, an Episcopal church. We crossed the line when we allowed Muslims to turn their backs on the cross of Christ and shout prayers that stated Allah is the greatest and is the one true God.

4. THEY DESPISED THEIR HERITAGE (Psalm 106:24)

How many Christians in America today are ashamed of their Christianity and show it through their compromises? How many have fallen away from their Christian/Jewish roots simply because we are more and more in the minority?

5. THEY COMPROMISED THEIR CHARACTER TO BE LIKE OTHERS (Psalm 106:28)

To fit in, Christians have been compromising their values and beliefs under the guise of tolerance. But the truth is: *What we tolerate we can't change.* Compromises are an excuse for disobedience. During the time of the Prophet Samuel, the ancient Hebrews asked for a king to rule over them, since Samuel was getting timeworn.

The prophet was greatly disappointed. So, he inquired of the Lord about what to do. The following is what the Bible records about it.

1 Samuel 8 (NIV)
Israel Asks for a King – America Asks for Big Government

"When Samuel grew old, he appointed his sons as Israel's leaders. The name of his firstborn was Joel and the name of his second was Abijah, and they served at Beersheba. But his sons did not follow his ways. They turned aside after dishonest gain and accepted bribes and perverted justice.

So all the elders of Israel gathered together and came to Samuel at Ramah. They said to him, "You are old, and your sons do not follow your ways; now appoint a king to lead us, such as all the other nations have."

But when they said, "Give us a king to lead us," this displeased Samuel; so he prayed to the LORD. *And the* LORD *told him: "Listen to all that the people are saying to you; it is not you they have rejected, but they have rejected me as their king. As they have done from the day I brought them up out of Egypt until this day, forsaking me and serving other gods, so they are doing to you. Now listen to them, but warn them solemnly and let them know what the king who will reign over them will claim as his rights."*

Samuel told all the words of the LORD *to the people who were asking him for a king. He said, "This is what the king who will reign over you will claim as his rights: He will take your sons and make them serve with his chariots and horses, and they will run in front of his chariots. Some he will assign to be commanders of thousands and commanders of fifties, and others to plow his ground and reap his harvest, and still others to make weapons of war and equipment for his chariots. He will take your daughters to be perfumers and cooks and bakers. He will take the best of your fields and vineyards and olive groves and give them to his attendants.*

He will take a tenth of your grain and your vintage and give it to his officials and attendants. Your male and female servants and the best of your cattle and donkeys he will take for his use. He will take a tenth of your flocks, and you yourselves will become his slaves. When that day comes, you will cry out for relief from the king you have chosen, but the LORD *will not answer you in that day." But the people refused to listen to Samuel. "No!" they said. "We want a king over us. Then we will be like all the other nations, with a king to lead us and to go out before us and fight our battles." When Samuel heard all that the people said, he repeated it before the*

LORD. *The LORD answered, "Listen to them and give them a king."*

Then Samuel said to the Israelites, "Everyone go back to your own town."

Of course, America has a President, not a king. So Americans have been saying, "We want a big government that will take care of us. We want to be like everyone else." Like ancient Israel, many Americans have stated that they want a "nanny" government to provide for them and meet all of their needs, rather than praying and seeking God for their provision. After all, big government will let us do what we want to do and say what we want to say and live like we want to live.

The attitudes of ancient Israel and modern America are strikingly similar. Israel wanted a King to take care of them, and many Americans want a big Socialist government to take of them. And in summary, like Deuteronomy 28 states, if we will sow what God says to sow (righteous seed) and where God says to plant it, we'll enjoy great blessings and success. But if we sow a seed that is not what God said to sow (unrighteous seed), we'll reap curses, poverty, and diseases.

Although Americans don't have a king, we're making the same mistakes as ancient Israel did when they rejected God's kingdom and embraced another kingdom – a human-made kingdom that makes promises it can't keep – fool's gold. American Christians who want big government to take care of them are compromising the word, the will and the ways of God because God alone is our provider. God alone is our King. He is far superior to any human government, and his provision is far beyond what we could even ask or think.

> **Wisdom Key:**
> **What you compromise climbing up the mountain of success will be your downfall at the top. (Bill Winston)**

Here's a list of the sins of Israel.
Can you see the parallels with America?

1. THEY TEMPTED GOD (Psalm 106:32)

The Israelites disobeyed God time and time again.

2. THEY REBELLED AGAINST THE HOLY SPIRIT (Psalm 106:33)

The Bible clearly teaches that we get our power and strength to fight temptation from the Holy Spirit. However, there is a staggering amount of people and churches that do not believe in or even teach about the Holy Spirit. Satan has rendered American Christians ineffective by taking away their source of power. Somewhere along the way, Christians compromised their beliefs and allowed the Holy Spirit's role to be reduced into a mystical-intellectual religious experience, rather than a close relationship between obedient sons of a loving Heavenly Father.

And today, in hopes of uniting Muslims, Jews, and Christians, Christians are being asked to compromise. The Bible calls this the end-time "apostate church". Remember this Wisdom Key: "What you compromise climbing up the mountain, will be your downfall at the top."

3. THEY REFUSED TO CARRY OUT GOD'S ORDERS (Psalm 106:34)

American Christians have a big problem with obedience. Compromise is just another way to justify disobedience.

4. THEY DEFILED THEMSELVES WITH EVIL (Psalm 106:39)

Many American Christians today look and act the same as the world. According to national polls, the divorce rates for Christians and non-Christians are about the same. Could it be that many Americans are being deceived by what I call "easy-believe-ism"?

Jesus commanded believers to make disciples of nations. At no time did Jesus create or encourage an institutional approach to "church membership" or focus on a 'Ya'll come!' mindset as we say in Texas. His focus was the Kingdom of God and a 'Ya'll go' mindset. The Great Commission says to "Go" and to "make disciples of all nations." But many have embraced the Old Testament paradigm that was to build a "temple" (church building) for God to dwell in and compel others to come to the House of God and experience the presence of God. However, the presence of God is manifested in the New Covenant through the followers of Christ. So, wherever believers go, the presence of God is there.

Like the Prophet Jeremiah said in Chapter 31, verse 33, "*...this shall be the covenant that I will make with the house of Israel; After those days, saith the LORD, I will put my law in their inward parts, and write it in their hearts; and will be their God, and they shall be my people.*"

It was not the "Gentiles" that brought down Israel/Judah.

It was the "Chosen Ones."
And it will not be the corrupt politicians that will bring down America.
It will be the Christians.
But, it's not too late!

In the book of Isaiah, we see another list of things the Israelites had done to cause their destruction. Can you see the parallels between Israel and America today?

- ✓ Their sacrifices were not heartfelt and in vain (Isaiah 1:13-5).
- ✓ They were corrupted by their love of money (Isaiah 1:23).
- ✓ They were selfish and only thought of themselves (Is. 1:23).
- ✓ They took up pagan practices (worshiped other gods and idols (Is. 2:6, 8-9).
- ✓ Their nation wanted for nothing (full of excess) (Is. 2:7).
- ✓ They were a prideful nation, lofty and haughty (Is. 2:17).
- ✓ Their tongues were against God (Is. 3:8).
- ✓ They did not hide their sins, much like Sodom. (Is. 3:9)
- ✓ Their leaders led them astray (Is. 3:12)
- ✓ The women dressed provocatively, trying to lure men (Is. 3:16-17)

Perhaps you can now see that America is on the same path of destruction as ancient Israel? And we will suffer the same devastating consequences if we don't turn back to God by complying with 2 Chronicles 7:14. But, there is hope! I believe America is about to be reborn.

Like during the times of Elijah, Elisha, and Jehu in 2 Kings 8-10, America is being positioned to expel the Spirit of Jezebel and Ahab stronghold in American government that has been increasing in power and influence since the early 1990's.

So how did Ahab and Jezebel come into power?

King David had been absent from the scene of Hebrew history for about 135 years when this story opens. (It has been 240 years since America's founding fathers first penned the Declaration of Independence.) His great kingdom, enlarged and more richly endowed by his son Solomon, had been fractured into two weakened fragments. The southern kingdom of Judah was being ruled by his descendants, while the northern kingdom of Israel suffered under a succession of corrupt leaders. One of them was King Ahab.

He is introduced with these stunning and remarkable words: "And Ahab the son of Omri did evil in sight of the Lord more than all who were before him" (1

Kings 16:30). He had the dubious distinction of being the 'most wicked' king who reigned over Israel. 1 Kings 16:31 says, *"And it came about, as though it had been a trivial thing for him to walk in the sins of Jeroboam the son of Nebat, that he married Jezebel the daughter of Ethbaal king of the Sidonians, and served and worshiped Baal."*

The Jezebel Connection

"Sidonians" was another name for the Phoenicians, a seafaring people on the Mediterranean coast who occupied the great cities of Tyre and Sidon. With the ever-present menace of Syria and the growing threat of Assyria, Ahab decided that he needed an alliance with this neighboring nation, so he made a treaty with the king of Phoenicia and sealed it by marrying his daughter. That is how Jezebel happened to move to Samaria, the capital of Israel, and there is only one way to describe it — *a whirlwind hit Israel.*

The king of Phoenicia was not only the political leader of his people, but he was also the high priest of their religion, as his name Ethbaal implies. Jezebel had grown up steeped in the worship of Baal and his female consort, Astarte (or Ashtoreth). Baal was considered to be the god of the *land.* According to the Phoenicians, he owned it, and he controlled its weather and the increase of its crops and cattle. Ashtoreth was considered to be the mother-goddess of fertility. So idols of both Baal and Ashtoreth stood side by side in their temples and were worshiped by priests and temple prostitutes with lewd dances and sacred orgies, with the hope that their god and goddess would follow their example and increase the productivity of their agriculture, their animals, and their children. In times of crisis such as famine, they slashed themselves and even sacrificed their children to appease the gods and implore their help.

Jezebel was fanatical about her religion. The worship of Yahweh (God) must have seemed dull and commonplace by comparison, and she was determined to change it. She was a headstrong, self-willed, domineering woman, and with a moral weakling for a husband, she had little trouble getting her way. She got him to build a house for Baal beside the palace in Samaria, as well as an "Ashtoreth," that is, an idol of the fertility goddess. Then she brought 450 prophets of Baal and 400 prophets of Ashtoreth from Phoenicia, housed them in the palace, and fed them in royal style. Their duties would have been to promote the worship of Baal and Ashtoreth throughout the land.

Not satisfied to just establish her religion in Israel, Jezebel sought to stamp out every remnant of Yahweh worship and to kill every true prophet of God. She had to have things completely her way, and she almost succeeded. Some prophets survived by compromising their convictions and turning into "yes" men for Ahab.

Where Are All the True Prophets?

A group of 100 Prophets was hidden in a cave and fed secretly by a godly servant of Ahab named Obadiah. But Elijah was the only one courageous enough to stand up *openly* against Jezebel's wickedness. God gave him a great victory when he called down fire from heaven upon Mount Carmel. The prophets of Baal were slain, and it looked as though the nation would turn back to God. But Jezebel was not finished with her evil work. She swore in her rage that she would kill Elijah, and he ran for his life, collapsing in the wilderness under a juniper tree, and pleading with God to let him die. It was the lowest point in the holy prophet's great career. And Baal worship lived on, dragging the nation to new depths of degradation. This stubborn, headstrong, self-willed wife of Ahab brought disruption and distress to Israel for many years to come.

Marriages to stubborn, willful people can bring unhappiness to all concerned. Their indomitable self-will which has never been surrendered to God will seldom give in to those around them. With unyielding obstinacy, they keep demanding their way and looking for every possible means and method of doing or having what they want. They will not listen to reason; they will not consider the feelings of others; they will not face the potential consequences of their intended actions. They believe that they are right and others are wrong, and they are determined to have everything their way. They obviously have a myopic view of God's love which "does not seek its own" (1 Cor. 13:5), but have only self-love which insists on its rights and demands its way.

Those who live with people like this eventually find themselves emotionally destroyed. For the survival of those around us, for the happiness of our mates and harmony in our marriages, we must face up to every trace of stubborn self-will and claim God's grace to deal with it.

Of course, Ahab was just as self-willed as Jezebel, but with a different temperament. For one thing, he had willfully entered a marriage that was politically convenient, but contrary to every word from God.

And Ahab's self-will becomes more evident in an incident involving *the king and his vegetable garden.*

Shortly after his marriage to Jezebel, Ahab not only beautified the palace at Samaria so that it came to be called "the ivory house" (1 Kings 22:39), but he also built a second palace in Jezreel. The second palace was twenty-five miles to the north, in an area of a more moderate climate in the wintertime. "Now it came about after these things, that Naboth the Jezreelite had a vineyard which was in Jezreel beside the palace of Ahab King of Samaria" (1 Kings 21:1).

Ahab decided he wanted Naboth's property. So he went to Naboth and said, "Give me your vineyard, which I may have it for a vegetable garden. I want it because it is close to my house, and I will give you a better vineyard than it in its place; if you like, I will give you the price of it in money" (1 Kings 21:2). Naboth declined the offer, just as he should have done, for God had forbidden the Jews to sell their paternal inheritance (Lev. 25:23-34). Naboth was merely obeying the law of the Lord.

"So Ahab came into his house sullen and vexed because of the word which Naboth the Jezreelite had spoken to him ... And he lay down on his bed and turned away his face and ate no food" (1 Kings 21:4).

Can you believe that a grown man would act this childishly? Maybe you have known someone like this? Weak, vacillating people like Ahab often want their way just as much as headstrong, domineering people like Jezebel. But they react differently when they do not get their way. While the powerful ones rant and rave, strike out at those who stand in their way, throw fits and destroy things, the weak ones sulk and pout and fret like spoiled children. They may refuse to get out of bed and even refuse to eat. They just want to feel sorry for themselves and let everybody know how bad things are for them. All they succeed in doing is letting people know how self-centered and immature they are.

Self-will that is violent or passive can ruin a marriage or any relationship. The trouble often starts when our mates infringe upon our sacred rights. Maybe the husband will not let his wife buy something she thinks she has a right to have, or the woman prepares an awful dinner on the very day hubby is expecting his favorite dish. Instead of letting the love and graciousness of Jesus Christ control us, our sinful natures take over, and we go into our rage routine or sulking syndrome. And it gradually eats away at our relationships. That inflexible self-will, which has never been broken and yielded to God, may ultimately lead to much more severe consequences. I have heard some say, "I don't love her anymore. I don't want her. I'm going to find some happiness for myself. And I don't care what the Bible says." The same thing can happen to our relationship with God and others, if we don't seek God and his kingdom first.

Like a trainer breaking a wild horse, God wants to break our sinful, stubborn wills. He desires to conquer them with his love. The first step to victory is simply to admit that continually demanding our way is disobedience to God's Word and therefore sin. Talk to the Lord about it and be candid with him. Tell him frankly that you would rather have your way than be unselfish and considerate of others, but acknowledge that it is contrary to his Word. Ask him to help you. Then by an act of your will, determine to do the loving thing. That step of faith will open the channel of God's power. He will not only enable you to carry through with your decision to act in love, but he will give you genuine delight. That is one big reason why Jesus sent us the Spirit of God.

But the Helper, the Holy Spirit, whom the Father will send in my name, he will teach you all things and bring to your remembrance all that I have said to you (Jesus) (John 14: 26).

King Ahab the Pouter

Let's go back to Ahab and his vegetable garden for a moment. Jezebel found Ahab sulking in his bed and asked him, "How is it that your spirit is so sullen that you are not eating food?" (1 Kings 21:5). So he explained to her how Naboth refused to let him have his vegetable garden. She replied, "Do you now reign over Israel?" (1 Kings 21:7). In modern terms, that might sound more like, "What are you, a man or a mouse? Squeak up! Don't you know that you are the king? You can take anything you want." With her Phoenician background, Jezebel could not seem to understand that even the King of Israel was subject to the laws of God.

We discover how thoroughly this weak and wicked man was dominated by his overbearing wife when she said, "Arise, eat bread, and let your heart be joyful; I will give you the vineyard of Naboth the Jezreelite" (1 Kings 21:7). She planned to commit a hideous crime.

Jezebel planned to pay two false witnesses to testify that they heard Naboth blaspheme God and the king, so that both Naboth and his sons would be stoned to death and the king would be free to lay claim to his land (2 Kings 9:26). Jezebel was going to teach Ahab her philosophy of life: "Take what you want and destroy anyone who stands in your way." And Ahab did not have the courage to stop her.

A man will do strange things when he is taunted and ridiculed by his wife. "Why didn't you stand up to him?" one woman jeered when she heard of her husband's latest disagreement with the boss. "When are you going to start acting like a man?" So the next time he did, and he lost his job, and everyone suffered. So the next round went like this: "You can't even provide for your family. What kind of a man are you?" So he showed her by roughing her up a little, and then by turning to cheating and stealing to make ends meet. And again, everyone in the family suffered.

A man needs respect from his wife, not ridicule. Of this shocking incident in Ahab's life, God said, "Surely there was no one like Ahab who sold himself to do evil in the sight of the Lord because Jezebel his wife incited him" (1 Kings 21:25). Some men need to be spurred on, to be sure, but not to do evil! A godly wife will challenge her husband to listen to God and live for him, not encourage him to sin.

You can't have a Jezebel without an Ahab

But the story is not over. These two were *self-willed to the end.* Elijah met Ahab in Naboth's vineyard and pronounced God's judgment on both him and Jezebel for their wicked deed. It was several years later when God's judgment came on Ahab, and it too is a story of self-will. The incident started over a city east of Jordan called Ramoth-Gilead, which Ahab said belonged to Israel but was still in the hands of Syria.

When Jehoshaphat, King of Judah, came to visit Ahab, he asked him if he would go to battle with him for Ramoth-Gilead. Jehoshaphat agreed but wanted to consult the Lord first. Ahab called his "yes" men together, and they assured him that the Lord would give Ramoth-Gilead into the hand of the king.

But Jehoshaphat was still not satisfied. He wanted another opinion: "Is there not yet a prophet of the Lord here that we may inquire of him?" (1 Kings 22:7). And Ahab replied, "There is yet one man by whom we may inquire of the Lord, but I hate him, because he does not prophesy good concerning me, but evil. He is Micaiah son of Imlah" (1 Kings 22:8).

Micaiah was called, and although he knew his life was in danger, he spoke what God told him. Israel would be scattered on the mountains like sheep without a shepherd (1 Kings 22:17). As we might expect, Ahab rejected Micaiah's prophecy and had him cast into prison. He was going to have what he wanted and do what he pleased, regardless of God's will.

The Death of Ahab

But it didn't work out quite like Ahab planned. He knew the Syrians would be after him, so he removed his royal garments and disguised himself as a regular soldier. "Now a certain man drew his bow at random and struck the king of Israel in a joint of the armor" (1 Kings 22:34). That soldier did not know he was shooting at the king, but his arrow penetrated the narrow slit between the pieces of Ahab's armor. Very few bowmen would have been that accurate. It was evident that God was guiding that arrow, and Ahab's self-will resulted in his untimely death.

Jezebel outlived him by almost fourteen years. Jehu, the captain of Israel's army, was to be the instrument of divine discipline in her case. After slaying King Jehoram, the son of Ahab, Jehu rode to Jezreel. Scripture says, "When Jehu came to Jezreel, Jezebel heard of it, and she painted her eyes and adorned her head, and looked out the window" (2 Kings 9:30). She knew what was about to happen, and she had decided that she was going to die like a queen, arrogant, self-willed and unrepentant to the end. She shouted abuses at Jehu from her upstairs window; but at Jehu's command, several of her servants threw her down, "and some of her blood was sprinkled on the wall and the horses, and he trampled her under foot" (2 Kings 9:33). It was a violent death, but it demonstrated the seriousness of sinful self-willed opposition to God.

Their influence lived on in their children. And this is often the saddest side effect of lives like Ahab's and Jezebel's. Two sons of Ahab and Jezebel later ruled in Israel. The first was Ahaziah. Of him, God says, "And he did evil in the sight of the Lord and walked in the way of his father and in the way of his mother and in the way of Jeroboam the son of Nebat, who caused Israel to sin. So he served Baal and worshiped him and provoked the Lord God of Israel to anger according to all that his father had done" (1 Kings 22:52, 53).

The second son to reign was Jehoram. As Jehu rode to execute vengeance on the house of Ahab, Jehoram cried, "Is it peace, Jehu?" Jehu summed up Jehoram's reign with his reply: "What peace, so long as the harlotries of your mother Jezebel and her witchcrafts are so many?" (2 Kings 9:22).

Curses on the House of Ahab

Ahab and Jezebel also had a daughter, Athaliah, and she married another man named Jehoram, the son of Jehoshaphat, king of the southern kingdom of Judah. "And he walked in the way of the kings of Israel, just as the house of Ahab did (for Ahab's daughter was his wife), and he did evil in the sight of the Lord" (2 Chronicles 21:6). At Jehoram's death, his son by Athaliah became king of Judah.

"Ahaziah was twenty-two years old when he became king, and he reigned one year in Jerusalem. His mother's name was Athaliah, the granddaughter of Onui. He also walked in the ways of the house of Ahab, for his mother was his counselor to do wickedly. And he did evil in the sight of the Lord like the house of Ahab, for they were his counselors after the death of his father, to his destruction" (2 Chron. 22:2-4).

And the evil influences continued generation after generation until God began to "hear their prayers, forgive their sins and heal their land". As we will learn, the healing of Israel started when God spoke to Elijah who talked to Elisha, who talked to a son of the school of prophets, who then spoke to Jehu, a commander of King Ahab's army. Then, Jehu talked to various leaders in the corrupt government of Israel and eventually delivered the following words to Queen Jezebel:

He (Jehu) looked up at the window (of Jezebel) and called out, "Who is on my side? Who?" Two or three eunuchs looked down at him. "Throw her down!" Jehu said. So they threw her down, and some of her blood spattered the wall and the horses as they trampled her underfoot just as Elijah had foretold (2 Kings 9:33).

Galatians 6:7-8 summarizes what happens to those that think they can live according to their self-will and unbridled lust and greed without any accountability to God! *"Be not deceived, God is not mocked. For whatsoever a man soweth. that shall he also reap. If he sows to the flesh, he will reap corruption of his flesh. If he sows to the Spirit, he will of the Spirit reap everlasting life." (KJV)*

Chapter 3: The Legacy of a Prophet

The ministry of Elijah began during the reign of Ahab and continued through the reign of Ahaziah, which places him in the period from 874BC-852BC. Elisha comes to prominence during the reign of Ahaziah and then continues until the reign of King Johoash of Israel, which ended in 782BC. This period of the divided kingdom commenced in 930BC. It also places us in a time of tremendous political upheaval. Both prophets ministered primarily within the Northern Kingdom although both also had contact with the King of Judah of the Southern Kingdom. Elisha additionally had significant dealings with the Syrians.

The early reign of Ahab was characterized by material prosperity. Ahab followed the precepts of his father and built strong alliances based upon trade and intermarriage: specifically to Jezebel of Tyre and Sidon. During his reign, he defeated the Syrians, temporarily ending their raids, and the Moabites, making them a vassal state. Ahab's relationship with the Syrians had the effect of stalling the campaigns of Shalmaneser III of Assyria for four years.

Interestingly, the extreme turbulence of those times eventually resulted in Ahab forming an alliance with Judah to attack Syria. It was during that battle that

Ahab received the wound from which he would ultimately die.

Ahab was succeeded by Ahaziah who died within two years, leaving Jehoram to take the throne. That instability prompted Mesha of Moab to rebel. He was eventually crushed by a coalition of Israel and Judah but only after doing significant damage to the southwest of the country. Meanwhile, North Syria was on the move again. They started with raids and later launched a full-scale attack against Samaria, a campaign which they lost.

It was during a subsequent battle with Syria that Jehoram was wounded, after which Jehu began to overthrow the corrupt government of Jezebel and Ahab. According to 2 Kings 9, God commissioned Elijah, Elijah commissioned Elisha, and Elisha commissioned "a son of the prophets" from his "school of the prophets" (the school of the prophets was first mentioned during the Prophet Samuel's time) to anoint Jehu king.

Jehu did not directly take the throne, however; he embarked upon a full-scale destruction of the previous royal house and also killed King Ahaziah of Judah. Israel had lost its allies and most of its experienced leadership. Around this time the ever-strengthening Assyrians swept down through the region and then returned home, leaving the way for Syria to attack its weakened neighbor until Israel had only fifty horsemen and ten thousand foot soldiers.

Towards the end of Elisha's ministry, Israel again gained strength. They were able to defeat Judah after a failed alliance; and then, under Joash, they were able to recapture Aphek as they had done during the time of Ahab. The victory over Joash may well have signaled the end of an era for Syria, as Joash's son Jeroboam II was later able to capture Damascus.

From a Biblical perspective, however, the political turmoil was an outward manifestation of an inward problem - spiritual corruption. In fact, the alliances that appeared to be a stroke of genius on the part of the house of Omri came with a hefty price: religious compromise. While Jeroboam, son of Nebat, encouraged idolatry, it was Ahab under the influence of Jezebel that introduced the worship of Baal and the goddess Asherah. This was more than a cult that polluted; by the time of Elijah, there were only seven thousand men in Israel that had not accepted Baal worship. Therefore we can see that this period was characterized not simply by a fight for the political survival of Israel, but also by a battle for the very spiritual distinctive that made Israel the people of God.

How did Israel get so bad after being so good under King David?

As we learned in Chapter 2, King David's kingdom had split into two smaller nations. The southern kingdom of Judah was ruled by the descendants of David, while the people living in the northern kingdom of Israel had to endure a long line of evil rulers. One of them was the husband in the next marital relationship we want to study.

Throughout their history in the Promised Land, the children of Israel struggled with conflict among the tribes. The disunity went back all the way to the patriarch Jacob, who presided over a house divided. The sons of Leah and the sons of Rachel had their share of contention even in Jacob's lifetime (Genesis 37:1-11).

The contention among the half-brothers continued in the time of the judges. Benjamin (one of Rachel's tribes) took up arms against the other tribes (Judges 20). Israel's first king, Saul, was of the tribe of

Benjamin. When David was crowned king—David was from the tribe of Judah (one of Leah's tribes)—the Benjamites rebelled (2 Samuel 2–3).

After a long war, the frailty of the union was exposed, however, when David's son Absalom promoted himself as the new king and drew many Israelites away from their allegiance to David (2 Samuel 15). Significantly, Absalom set up his throne in Hebron, the site of the former capital (v. 10). A later revolt was led by a man named Sheba against David and the tribe of Judah (2 Samuel 20:1-2).

Israel - The Divided Kingdom

The reign of David's son Solomon saw more unrest when one of the king's servants, Jeroboam, rebelled. Jeroboam was on the king's errand when he met the prophet Ahijah who told him that God was going to give him authority over ten of the twelve tribes of Israel. God's reason for the division of the kingdom was definitive: "Because they have forsaken me and have not walked in my ways." However, God promised that David's dynasty would continue, albeit over a much smaller kingdom, for the sake of God's covenant with David and the three of Jerusalem, God's chosen city. When Solomon learned of the prophecy, he sought to kill Jeroboam, who fled to Egypt for sanctuary (1 Kings 11:26-40).

Israel Was Divided – North against the South
After Solomon's death, his son Rehoboam was set to become the next king. Jeroboam returned from Egypt and led a group of people to confront Rehoboam with a demand for a lighter tax burden. When Rehoboam refused the order, ten of the tribes rejected Rehoboam and David's dynasty (1 Kings 12:16), and Ahijah's prophecy was fulfilled. Only Judah and Benjamin remained loyal to King Rehoboam. The northern tribes crowned Jeroboam as their king.

Rehoboam made plans to mount an assault on the rebel tribes, but the Lord prevented him from taking that action (vv. 21-24). Meanwhile, Jeroboam further consolidated his power by instituting a form of calf worship unique to his kingdom and declaring that pilgrimages to Jerusalem were unnecessary. Thus, the people of the northern tribes would have no contact with the tribes of Judah and Benjamin.

"So Israel has been in rebellion against the house of David to this day" (1 Kings 12:19). The northern kingdom is called "Israel" (or sometimes "Ephraim") in Scripture, and the southern kingdom is called "Judah". From the divine viewpoint, the division was a judgment on not keeping God's commands, specifically the commands prohibiting idolatry. From a human perspective, the division was the result of tribal discord and political unrest. The principle is that sin brings division (1 Corinthians 1:13, 11:18; James 4:1). The good news is that God, in his mercy, has promised a reuniting of the northern and southern kingdoms. "He will raise a banner for the nations and gather the exiles of Israel; he will assemble the scattered people of Judah from the four quarters of the earth. Ephraim's jealousy will vanish, and Judah's enemies will be destroyed; Ephraim will not be jealous of Judah, nor Judah hostile toward Ephraim" (Isaiah 11:12-13). When the Prince of Peace—Jesus Christ—reigns in his millennial kingdom, all hostility, jealousy, and conflict among the tribes will be put to rest.

A Last Look at Ahab and Jezebel

Ahab and Jezebel were evil, and their influence lived on past their lifetimes. In America, God only knows how many generations will have been affected by our sinful self-will, our insistence on having things our way instead of God's.

What happened to the days of focusing on what the Spirit of God is saying, rather than what the latest popular author, pastor, denomination or college professor has written or said?

A Timeline of Elijah's Ministry

- Elijah tells Ahab there will be no rain for several years. (1 Kings 17:1)
- God tells Elijah to hide in the Kerith Ravine. (1 Kings 17:2)
- God commands him to go to a widow's house in Sidon. (1 Kg 17:9)
- Elijah heals the widow's son. (1 Kings 17:21)
- God tells Elijah to present himself to Ahab. (1 Kings 18:1)
- Obadiah meets Elijah. (1 Kings 18:7)
- Ahab goes with Obadiah to meet Elijah. (1 Kings 18:16)
- Elijah challenges Ahab's prophets at Mount Carmel. (1 Kings 18:19)
- Elijah has the prophets of Baal killed. (1 Kings 18:40)
- Elijah summons rain from on top of Mount Carmel. (1 Kings 18:45)
- The spirit of the Lord comes over Elijah, and he runs to Jezreel (1 Kings 18:46)
- Elijah flees from Jezebel. (1 Kings 19:1)
- An Angel of the Lord feeds Elijah. (1 Kings 19:4)
- The Lord asks Elijah why he is hiding. (1 Kings 19:9)

- The Lord sends Elijah to anoint Hazael king of Aram. (1 Kings 19:15)
- The Lord sends Elijah to anoint Jehu king of Israel. (1 Kings 19:16)
- The Lord sends Elijah to anoint Elisha as a prophet. (1 Kings 19:16)
- Elijah anoints Elisha as a prophet. (1 Kings 19:19)
- God sends Elijah to deliver a prophecy of death to Ahab. (1 Kings 21:17)
- Elijah prophesies the death of Jezebel. (1 Kings 21:23)
- God tells Elijah that he has postponed the death of Ahab. (1 Kings 21:28)
- Ahab dies as GOD had told Elijah. (1 Kings 22:34)
- Ahaziah, son of Ahab, becomes king of Israel. (1 Kings 22:51)
- Elijah sends a message to Ahaziah that he will die in bed. (2 Kings 1:3)
- Ahaziah sends troops to kill Elijah. (2 Kings 1:9)
- God sends Elijah to Ahaziah. (2 Kings 1:15)
- Ahaziah dies as God said he would. (2 Kings 1:17)
- Joram becomes King of Israel. (2 Kings 1:17)
- God takes Elijah to heaven in a chariot of fire. (2 Kings 2:11)
- Elisha receives the double anointing as promised (2 Kings 2:9-10)

Chapter 4: Double for Your Trouble

Reading the life and works of the prophet Elisha superficially, one is quickly disappointed. He does not seem to measure up to our expectations of a prophet. Where do we find in him the moral indignation of Nathan, who daringly confronted David over his sin with Bathsheba; or the fury of Elijah with Ahab for the murder of Naboth; or the passion for justice and righteousness of the literary prophets? And yet, 9 out of 25 chapters of the Book of 2nd Kings are devoted to Elisha's career, while the remaining 16 chapters deal with no fewer than 13 kings of Israel (a span of approximately 132 years until its destruction in 722 BC) and 17 kings of Judah (a span of about 289 years until its destruction in 586 BC).

How do we explain this disparity? There can be no question that the author of the Book of Kings was from the prophetic school – Talmudic (Rabbinic) tradition - which asserts that Jeremiah wrote it. For Jeremiah, the career of kings was of secondary, even fleeting, importance and he was impressed with the achievements of Elisha. Still, as suggested in the previous paragraph, a superficial analysis of the relevant chapters leaves most readers with the impression of a hodge-podge of loosely connected episodes centered on Elisha.

However, a more careful study reveals a pattern from which emerges a remarkable man who dedicated his life to one goal: the total elimination of Baal-worship in Israel.

We will note Elisha's growth from a disciple of Elijah to the undisputed leader of the disciples of prophets; his influence on royalty; his high reputation beyond the borders of Israel in Aram; and, his crowning achievement, the toppling of the House of Omri. All this is told by a master narrator who learned his skill from the author of the Book of Samuel.

From Disciple to Successor

Elijah's feat of faith on Mt. Carmel, where all the prophets of Baal were put to the sword (1 Kings 18:20-46), brought him only anguish and frustration, and a threat to his life by the evil Jezebel, consort of King Ahab. Tired of living, he begged the Lord to take his life. Elijah fled to Mt. Horeb, where he was charged with three missions: anoint Hazael to rule over Aram, Jehu to be king over Israel, and Elisha to be the prophet in his stead (19:15-16). Of the three mandates, Elijah only implemented the last one himself.

Elijah found Elisha ben-Shaphat from Abel-meholah plowing with 12 oxen. Elisha went unhesitatingly with Elijah and ministered to him (19:21). It is not stated how long Elisha served as Elijah's disciple; but it is told that he witnessed the sudden appearance of a fiery chariot with horses that took Elijah up to heaven in a whirlwind (2 Kings 2:11). Elisha received a double anointing that enabled him to perform twice as many miracles as Elijah. A band of the school of prophets from Jericho, who had been watching from a distance, noticed Elisha donning the mantle of Elijah and came to meet him and bowed down before him (2:15). Elijah assumed leadership over them. His reputation as a man of God was fully established when he cured the poisoned waters in Jericho (2:19-22), and when he caused the death of little children who had dared to mock him (2:23).

I cannot imagine a greater contrast in personality than that of Elijah and Elisha. Elijah was a loner. We are aware of the existence of roving bands of the school of the prophets. We know of Obadiah, a prominent official in the service of King Ahab, who saved 100 prophets of the Lord from the fury of

Jezebel by hiding and sustaining them in two caves (1 Kings 18:13). We know of no instance in which Elijah made contact with any one of them, or even that he was aware of their existence. He certainly seemed unaware of them when he complained on Mt. Horeb that "the children of Israel have ... slain thy prophets and I, even I only, am left".

In contrast, Elisha assumed leadership of the school of prophets, ate with them (2 Kings 4:38-44), helped them to enlarge their abode (6:1-7), and performed miracles for those who were his loyal followers (4:1-7; 4:8-37). In all probability, he also created new cells of the school of the prophets to serve as teachers, exhorting people to serve the Lord. Who were these disciples of the prophets and what was their function?

We meet them for the first time when Saul, having been secretly anointed by Samuel to be king in Israel, is told "... Thou shalt meet a band of prophets with a psaltery, and a timbrel, and a pipe, and a harp, before them" (1 Sam. 10:5). Later on, we read of the company of the prophets prophesying and Samuel standing as the leader over them (19:20). As disciples of the prophets, they came into prominence in the life of Elisha. From this rather scant record, one can make an educated guess about their function. Established by Samuel and trained by him in the rudiments of Israel's faith, they passed through the land and "prophesied" accompanied by musical instruments. That is, as enthusiasts, they attempted to wean the people from idol worship and to strengthen their faith in the Lord.

Elijah was a tragic figure during his lifetime. He was constantly in flight, in fear of his life. His great success on Mt. Carmel, where he convinced Israel of the might of the Lord and the powerlessness of Baal, had no lasting results. In contrast, Elisha succeeded in all his undertakings, and his fame as "wonderworker" or "man of God" spread throughout Israel and beyond it. While the great Elijah was insulted by King Ahab of Israel, Elisha was sought by Jehoram and Jehoshaphat, kings of Israel and Judah respectively, to help them in moments of great need. Elisha was visited by Naaman, commander of the army of Aram, to heal him of leprosy; and was visited shortly before his death by King Jehoash of Israel. It was only after his death that Elijah was revered by Israel as the harbinger of the final redemption. Malachi, the last of the Hebrew prophets, closed his prophetic book with "Behold I will send you Elijah the prophet before the coming of the great and terrible day of the Lord." In the final judgment, Elijah became the man of eternity while Elisha was portrayed as the man of the hour.

Growing Influence

In the year 1868 AD, the Moabite Stone was discovered. In its inscriptions, Mesha, King of Moab, tells of his successful rebellion against the King of Israel. The same event appears in 2 Kings 3, broadly corresponding to that of the Moabite Stone. King Jehoram of Israel made an alliance with King Jehoshaphat of Judah and the King of Edom, to put down the rebellion. The road of the allied armies led through the wilderness of Edom. They marched for seven days, rounding the tip of the Dead Sea, and no water was left for men and animals. At this moment of great despair, Jehoshaphat requested the presence of a prophet who could inquire of the Lord. So the King of Israel and Jehoshaphat and the King of Edom went down to him [Elisha] (2 Kings 3:12).

Elisha prophesied that a *wadi* would be filled with water and that Moab would be delivered into their hands. After some initial military successes of the allies, the King of Moab, in desperation, sacrificed his firstborn on the walls of his city, after which "a great wrath" came upon Israel. The alliance was broken up, and each member withdrew to his land. It can be stated with good reason that, were it not for the involvement of Elisha; this entire event would not have been recorded in the Book of Kings. This episode, if properly analyzed, was told to indicate the growing prominence of Elisha.

The author, ill-disposed toward Israelite kings, most subtly enables us to compare this story to what happened years back, during the reign of King Ahab, as related in 1 Kings 22. At that time, King Jehoshaphat of Judah, on a visit to Ahab, was asked by the latter to join him to reconquer Ramoth-Gilead from the Arameans. The false prophet Zedekiah ben-Chenaanah made himself horns of iron to demonstrate that in such fashion the two kings would "gore" the Arameans. On the insistence of Jehoshaphat, Micaiah, a true prophet, was summoned before them. After some hesitation, Micaiah prophesied defeat. Thereupon Zedekiah smote Micaiah on the cheek, and as if this crude insult were not enough, Ahab ordered that he be put in prison and fed scant bread with only scarce water until Ahab came in peace (1 Kings 22:28).

Elisha, by contrast, was afforded a highly respectable treatment by royalty. In fact, 2 Kings 3:12, where the King of Israel and Jehoshaphat and the King of Edom went down to Elijah, has not been given sufficient attention. It seems to point to an essential ingredient in Elisha's personality. Not only does he meet royalty, but *they also come to him*.

No wonder that the author of the Book of Kings held Elisha in such high regard. The true prophet, the messenger of God, wields spiritual authority far above those who have worldly power. This interpretation of the real significance of this entire episode gains unexpected poignancy by the fact that, in the final analysis, the prophecy of Elisha was not fulfilled. The failure of the military enterprise is summed up in the mysterious phrase "a great wrath came upon Israel", without specifying who was angered, and why this anger was directed at Israel.

International Reputation

It was a young Israelite girl, captured by roving Aramean bands and brought into the household of Naaman, who was responsible for spreading the fame of Elisha beyond the borders of Israel. Naaman suffered from the dreadful disease of leprosy, and in her naiveté, this young girl told her mistress, "I wish the master could come before the prophet in Samaria, for he could cure him of it" (2 Kings 5:3). Naaman repeated the information to his King, who promptly dispatched him with a letter to the King of Israel, stating, "When this letter reaches you, know that I have sent my courier Naaman to you, that you may cure him of his leprosy" (5:6).

When the King of Israel read the letter, he ripped his clothes, fearing that the King of Aram was seeking a pretext against him. On hearing about it, Elisha sent a message to the King requesting that Naaman "come to [him], so he will learn that there is a prophet in Israel" (5:8). Naaman then came with horses and chariots to the house of Elisha who, instead of welcoming him, informed him by a messenger to go and bathe seven times in the Jordan River. It seems that Naaman may have expected a mighty spectacle by the prophet and the use of magic, and probably annoyed by the standoffish attitude of Elisha, stalked off in a rage. It was only at the urging of his servants that he did what Elisha had bidden him do, and he was cured.

Elated and a changed man, Naaman returned to Elisha, acknowledging that "there is no God in the whole world except in Israel" (5:15). Naaman asked to take two mule-loads of earth with him to Aram, on which he would offer sacrifices to the Lord alone. Then he added: "But may the Lord pardon your servant for this when my master [the King of Aram] enters the temple of Rimon ... And he is leaning on my arm so that I must bow low ... may the Lord pardon your servant in this" (5:18). This episode in Elisha's life, briefly told and masterfully written, contains three layers of significance, not recorded, but left to the creative interpretation of the reader.

First, we again note Elisha maintaining the principled stance of the prophet and man of God who towers above men holding worldly power. Naaman came down twice to Elisha. The second has religious implications. It is the second instance of conversion recorded in the Bible, the first being that of Ruth the Moabitess.

Elisha, a true prophet in Israel, must have indicated that Naaman's cure was not accomplished by magic but by the power of Yahweh (God). Finally, the healing of Naaman served as a stepping stone in Elisha's rise to fame, enabling him as a "kingmaker" to implement his inner strivings to eliminate Baal-worship in Israel.

The Kingmaker

It is not clear why Elisha was mandated to anoint Hazael to rule over Aram (8:7-15). However, the choice of Jehu to topple the House of Omri is evident. He was an uncompromising loyalist of the Lord, who would wage a relentless war against Baal. Ahab, under the influence of his wife Jezebel, a Phoenician princess, had erected an altar to Baal in a temple he built in Samaria. So deeply embedded was this idol-worship in the House of Omri that Ahaziah, son of Ahab, mortally injured when he fell through a lattice of his upper chamber, sent messengers to inquire of Beelzebub, god of Ekron, whether he would recover.

Elijah, in his relentless struggle against Baal, had caused the slaying of the prophets of Baal on Mt. Carmel. However, Elisha fully understood that this was not the proper or most effective approach. To eliminate Baal, one had to go to the very source of this evil and root out those responsible for importing his prophets.

Jehu's military coup, described most dramatically in 2 Kings 9-10, was successful. In a bloody and ruthless campaign, which led to the defenestration (throwing out of a window) of the hated Jezebel, he not only eradicated the House of Omri but also the "Baal of Israel." Fifty years of Elisha's eventful life came to an end. In a touching scene, King Joash [Jehoash], grandson of Jehu, came to him, crying, "My father, my father, the chariots of Israel and the horsemen thereof" (13:14), reminiscent of the words that Elisha had addressed to the vanishing Elijah (2:12).

Additional Thoughts

The bloody and cruel rebellion of Jehu may have led to disappointment and even to revulsion. The prophetic author of the Book of Kings, so pleased with the downfall of the House of Omri, credited Jehu with his feat: Thus Jehu eradicated Baal worship from Israel (10:28).

Nevertheless, he leveled severe criticism at him when he said, "And Jehu took no heed to walk in the law of the Lord with all his heart. He departed not from the sins of Jeroboam, which he made Israel sin" (10:31).

After about 50 years, a new type of literary prophet burst upon the scene, beginning with Amos and Hosea. They created an unprecedented spiritual revolution. It may have dawned on this new kind of prophet that the ways of Elijah and Elisha were not the most efficient ones – at least during their time.

As God's messenger, a prophet was obliged to bring God's message to the people, educating them by speech and written words, addressing himself directly to their consciences. Though not always successful in their own time, the orations of profound moral instruction of these prophets would become the heritage of all humankind. The legacy of those prophets lives to this very day.

END-TIME OBJECTIVE

To enable heaven to invade earth as the Priestly and Kingly anointings become one! (Revelation 1:6 and Revelation 5:10).

"And hath made us kings and priests unto God and his Father; to him be glory and dominion forever and ever. Amen" (Revelation 1:6).

"And hast made us unto our God kings and priests: and we shall reign on the earth" (Revelation 5:10).

The idea of "two anointings becoming one" is personified in the Elisha end-time: double anointing! God is looking for Elishas to prophesy to the Jehus to "throw her (the spirit of Jezebel and Ahab) down" underneath our feet. Notice in 2 Kings that Ahab (the enabler) was defeated before Jezebel was overcome. I believe that's a message for us today. You can't have a Jezebel without an Ahab!

I believe that the Spirit of Jezebel is a ruling spirit that must have a Spirit of Ahab in which to operate. The Ahab Spirit is the door which the Jezebel Spirit must use to usurp God's authority and become a stronghold. We can scream and yell or bind/loose the Jezebel Spirit until we're blue in the face. But if we don't defeat and dethrone the enabling Spirit of Ahab, we will never be able to dethrone and throw down the Spirit of Jezebel. Can you see this?

We may ask, "Where are the Jehus?" But God is asking, "Where are the Elishas? And where are the ones that are willing to pray and pay the price for my anointing?"

Have you ever heard of "The Great Omission"?

Is that a typo? You are probably asking, "Don't you mean the Great *Commission*?" You remember, don't you? The Great Commission as spoken by Jesus Christ. It's traditionally defined as the primary mission of the New Testament Church. As you may also know, it has been widely taught that every believer in Christ should be involved in "sharing the plan of salvation" (also called the "Gospel of Jesus Christ") with as many as possible. And as enough people accept Christ as their personal Savior, a new church would be started and lives would be changed.

As a young teenage Christian, I can remember when I was taught to share the plan of salvation with someone and lead them in the prayer of salvation, thinking that my God-given responsibilities were completed; but were they? Have you ever done that or felt that way? Is that really what the Great Commission says in Matthew 28? I've discovered that some things have been forgotten and therefore omitted. That's why I'm talking about "The Great *Omission*," rather than the Great *Commission*.

As a result of this way of looking at the Great Commission over the past 100 years, some American evangelical churches have grown in significant numbers. But have their lives been changed? And have they changed their culture? Have they been preaching repentance? Or perhaps many have been teaching an easy-believe-ism and sloppy-agape gospel? Many religious surveys have shown that divorce and other social maladies are just as bad in American evangelical churches as in the secular world. For example, in the USA, recent surveys have shown that around 75% of Americans call themselves "Christian," yet our public schools and federal government seem to be running away from anything that honors the God of the Bible or the Bible of the Christian God. Why is that?

One reason is that many Christians have trained their converts "to share the Gospel of Christ, get people saved and plant new churches," while thinking they are fulfilling the Great Commission. And by doing that, American Christians have believed that they were obedient to the words of Jesus as spoken in Matthew 28: 16-20. But is that what the Great Commission says in Matthew 28? And is that really what the Gospel of Christ is? And most of all, what does the Bible really say about the Great Commission and the Gospel of Jesus Christ?

In this chapter, I will attempt to answer those questions and try to help the body of Christ return to the simplicity of the Gospel of Jesus Christ, while fulfilling the Great Commission as taught by Jesus. As a young Christian, I had a more limited understanding of what the Great Commission of

Jesus Christ was. I thought that if I could just proclaim the Gospel to everyone, using tools like radio, television, and publications, I would have fully obeyed the Great Commission. But then I discovered Christ's teachings about the Kingdom of God.

The Kingdom Is Present and Future

Attempts to see the Kingdom of God as a future event are mostly the product of the late nineteenth century's rise of dispensationalists. The books of Matthew, Mark, Luke, and John tell us the Kingdom is to be sought in our lives and to be received now, that a man in Christ's day could see it and enter into it, and that it is found among us. Imposing a parenthetical "church age" into history to defer such references to an end-of-time eschatological millennium does not work, for Paul speaks of the Kingdom in the present tense, not just the future.

Other passages refer to the Kingdom as a progressive, developing fact. The Lord's Prayer petitions "Thy kingdom come," whereas we are told that "the kingdom of God has come" and that it is on earth and in heaven. Many of the parables regarding the Kingdom describe it in terms of the growth of a seed, tree, or yeast that develops over a period of time. These scriptures are in support of Genesis 8:22 where God declares, "As long as the earth remains, seedtime and harvest, cold and heat, summer and winter, day and night will never cease." I believe the words "seedtime and harvest" are a type and shadow of the coming Kingdom of God as preached by Jesus Christ and John the Baptist.

There is no denying that many references to the Kingdom are in the future as well as now. It is described as existing at the end of the world and after the final judgment. The angelic messenger told Mary it would have "no end" and the Epistles refer to it as "an everlasting kingdom" that is "forever and ever."

The Great Commission of Jesus is not just to preach the Gospel to the entire world, but also to make disciples of all nations. Let's look at what Matthew 28 says.

MATTHEW 28:18-20 (NKJ)

"Then Jesus came and spoke to them, saying, 'All authority has been given to me in heaven and on earth. Go therefore and make disciples of all the nations, baptizing them in the name of the Father

and of the Son and the Holy Spirit, teaching them to observe all things that I have commanded you; and lo, I am with you always, even to the end of the age."

As you can see, this passage mentions four things:

1. All authority was given to Jesus,

2. We are to make disciples of all nations,

3. Disciples should be baptized in the name of the Father, Son, and the Holy Spirit and

4. We are to teach those disciples to obey all that Jesus taught.

The Great Commission includes teaching disciples to do all the things Jesus taught his original disciples.

A commission is (1) authorization to perform certain duties, or to take on certain powers, (2) authority to act on behalf of another, (3) an entrusting, as of power, authority, etc., to a person/body.

When considering all of the words Jesus said and what he taught, he frequently said to the disciples to "follow me," not just accept me as Savior, or just pray this prayer after me. Further, I found that the Greek meaning of the words translated "believe" or "faith" referred to both mental assent/convictions and corresponding actions. Perhaps that was most clearly communicated in the book of James, "faith without works is dead."

For example, if you believe that a chair will hold you if you sit in it, then you will sit in the chair. But if you don't believe that the chair will hold you, then you won't sit in the chair. In summary, the "faith" that Jesus taught compelled the true believers to have corresponding actions in support of their particular beliefs, not merely mental assent.

In contrast, the Greeks during the time of Christ loved to meet and debate various philosophies while believing that actual knowledge was purely intellectual. If they could intelligently and persuasively discuss their points of view in public, then they were admired and revered. Some of the more famous Greeks who participated in this were Plato and Socrates. Many American educational philosophies that have been implemented in US Public Schools have their origins in Greek philosophy.

Can you see the difference between the Biblical meaning of faith and the Greek philosophical meaning of faith? The Greek Philosophy definition of faith was to give mental assent only to something, but the Biblical meaning of faith is to give mental assent along with corresponding actions in support of that belief. As the book of James teaches, "Faith without works is dead."

Jesus clearly taught that the Gospel of Jesus Christ is the Gospel of the Kingdom of God, referring to a new and greater governmental order of God in which heaven will/can invade earth and of which there will be no end. So, the Gospel (the good news) is that Jesus was legally returning everything back to humankind that was lost when Adam and Eve disobeyed in the Garden of Eden. This restoration of individual legal rights to all that will believe includes all three parts of man – body, soul, and spirit.

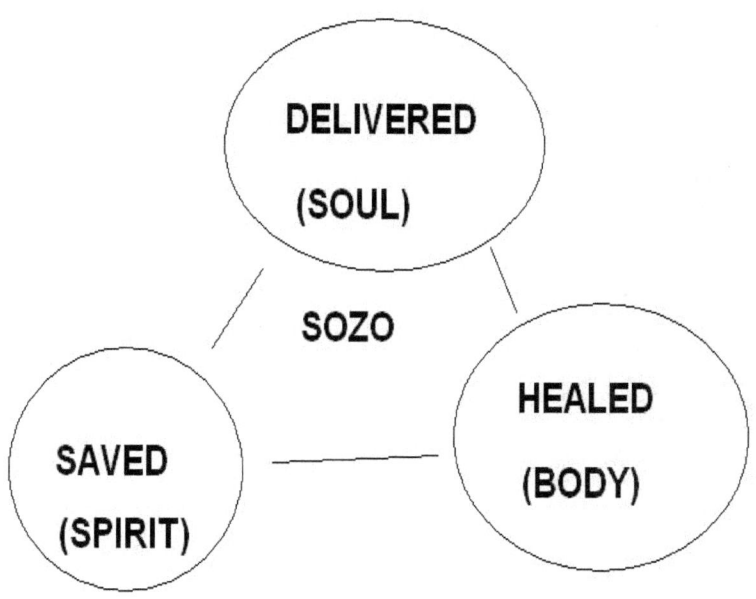

SOZO is the transliteration in English of the Greek word translated as saved and salvation as mentioned in the Bible. Notice that for every part of man that exists; Jesus made provision for our complete restoration on the cross. It is included in salvation. Jesus died for every part of us – body, soul and spirit. A complete translation of SOZO would be "to be made whole." And interestingly, some English translations translate it that way. Instead of Jesus declaring healing and miracles by saying "Be Healed!" Jesus is quoted saying, "Be made whole!" Although all won't be restored until the appointed time, we can enjoy as much of our inheritance in Christ as we have the faith to receive right now, because "faith is now."

The word SOZO (translated as 'salvation') has three parts to its meaning. It means Saved, Healed, and Delivered. *Saved* is referring to your spirit. Jesus died so that your spirit may be renewed and filled with the Holy Spirit, and you may enter into a relationship with the Father and enjoy eternal life. *Healed* is referring to your physical body. Jesus died so that your physical body may be healed. And *deliverance* is referring to your Soul. The Soul is comprised of the mind, will, and emotions. That is where addictions can occur. It is also where many of our traumas are stored. *Deliverance* is about freeing us from hurts, bondages, and addictions so that we don't have to be tormented anymore. That is one reason why it is called the good news (gospel) of Christ.

The Gospel of the Kingdom Is the Gospel of Jesus

When Jesus returned everything back to humanity that was lost when Adam and Eve disobeyed in the Garden of Eden, this restoration was for certain legal rights (heavenly inheritances) to all that will believe, including all three parts of man – body, soul, and spirit.

Matthews 6:33 says, "Seek ye first the Kingdom of God and his righteousness and all these other things will be added unto you..." Jesus has provided for us to have everything we need for our life-long journey to learn how to be all God wants us to be and to do all God wants us to do.

"And he (Jesus) said unto them, unto you is given to know the mystery of the kingdom of God: but unto them that are without, all *these* things are done in parables." (Mark 4:11)

A Hard Question

Are you able to discern the mysteries of the Kingdom of God? I pray so! I want to help you learn how to <u>be all</u> God wants you to be and <u>do all</u> God wants you to do. Of course, that is subject to your ability to discern and learn about the Kingdom of God.

The Mystery of the Kingdom

Colossians 1: 27, "To them God has chosen to make known among the Gentiles the glorious riches of this mystery, which is Christ in you, the hope of glory."

In Christ, we now have the potential to live free from bondage in our souls, oppression in our spirits and diseases in our bodies, while having all of our physical needs supplied. Matthew 6:33 says, "Seek first the Kingdom of God and his righteousness and all of these things will be added unto you."

The double anointing (empowerment) that Elisha received was a type of end-time anointing mentioned in the book of Revelation. That's why, I believe, that anointing was the combination of The Kingly and Priestly Anointings. Adam was given the double anointing of the Kingly and Priestly in the Garden of Eden.

The Spirit of Elijah (Elisha's mentor) is prophesied to return during the last days because Christ will have restored all things. The Elisha double anointing has been available for all who will believe it, receive it and activate it by faith.

I believe that Elijah had a Priestly anointing only because his assignment was to defeat all of the false prophets supporting Jezebel. However, Elisha got Elijah's Priestly anointing and a Kingly anointing - a double anointing.

We can only operate in the delegated authority that God has given us. I believe that's why Elijah prophesied to Elisha to prophesy to Jehu, although Elisha chose to send a son of the prophets to Jehu instead of going himself. It was all about God's delegated authority. Elijah prophesied to Elisha to prophesy to Jehu, a commander in Ahab's army, to get rid of Ahab and Jezebel. After that, Jehu would become the next King, indicating that God had delegated to Jehu a Kingly anointing to rule over Israel, but not a Priestly anointing. The Kingly (or royal) anointing brings earth to heaven. The Priestly anointing brings heaven to earth.

Jesus became the Lamb of God (Priestly anointing), and after the resurrection, Jesus became the Lion of Judah (Priestly anointing) – The King of Kings. That's why he's called the King of Kings *and* our High Priest. Jesus said, "So send I you," because we're also called to be kings and priests. Our Kingly authority enables us to rule and reign (take dominion) on earth, while the Priestly anointing enables us to be fruitful and multiply. That's why Jesus said in the Lord's Prayer: "Thy kingdom come. Thy will be done on earth as it is heaven…" The phrase "Thy kingdom come" is referring to our Kingly anointing and the words, "Thy will be done on earth as it is in heaven" are referring to our Priestly anointing. All of this is made possible by the death, burial and resurrection of Christ.

Elisha's double anointing empowered him to identify and oversee "a company or school of prophets" like I feel led to do (a type of Elisha) while honoring the Prophetic word from prior generations (like Dr. Bill Hamon - a type of Elijah). God wants us to stand on the shoulders of the previous generation to take the Kingdom of God to the next generation while experiencing a new level of God's glory.

To accomplish that, we need to understand and honor delegated authority, the Ancient Hebrew Model of Discipleship and the end-time Elisha double anointing to reign as kings and priests. Since Jesus has legally restored all that was lost through Adam and Eve, the double anointing will enable mankind to begin to fully accomplish God's original purpose for mankind – to take dominion, be fruitful and multiply. This is how heaven will fully invade earth.

Elisha took what Elijah taught, stood on Elijah's shoulders, and sent a son of the prophets under his leadership to cause King Ahab and Queen Jezebel to be defeated. I believe it took the double anointing (Kingly and Priestly) to overcome the passivity of Ahab and the manipulation of Jezebel. The same is true today.

I believe the Lord has shown me that the Republican Party establishment in the US is like Ahab and the Democratic Party is like Jezebel. God is going to prune American politics of these evil influences through the Elisha Company of Prophets – those that will qualify for the Elisha end-time double anointing with spiritual empowerment – who are being raised up right now the same way God used Elisha. Are you one of them?

If you are an Elisha (a leader that ministers to church and marketplace leaders), tell the Jehu's in your life that they need to bind up the Jezebel Spirit and loose the Kingdom of God, while overseeing the training of a school of prophetic people.

If you're a Jehu (a leader in the marketplace), start prophesying to the Ahab and Jezebel Spirits, telling them to get underneath your feet, while believing, receiving and activating the double anointing God has given you through Christ. God wants us to take righteous dominion on earth by activating the Kingly and Priestly anointings.

A Timeline of Elijah's Ministry

- Elijah instructed to anoint (1 Kings 19:16)
- Called by Elijah (1 Kings 19:19)
- Ministers to Elijah (1 Kings 19:21)
- Witnesses Elijah's translation, receives a double portion of his spirit (2 Kings 2:1-15; 2 Kings3:11)
- Mocked by the children of Bethel (2 Kings 2:23-24)
- Causes the king to restore the property of the hospitable *Shunammite* (2 Kings 8:1-6)
- Instructs that Jehu be anointed King of Israel (2 Kings 9: 1-3)
- Life of, sought by Jehoram (2 Kings 6:31-33)

- Death of Elisha (2 Kings 13:14-20)
- Bones of, restore a dead man to life (2 Kings 13:21)

Miracles of Elisha

- Divides the Jordan (2 Kings 2:14)
- Purifies the waters of Jericho by casting salt into the fountain (2 Kings 2:19-22)
- Increases the oil of the woman whose sons were to be sold for debt (2 Kings 4:1-7)
- Raises from the dead the son of the Shunammite (2 Kings 4:18-37)
- Neutralizes the poison of the pottage (2 Kings 4:38-41)
- Increases the bread to feed one hundred men (2 Kings 4:42-44)
- Heals Naaman the leper (2 Kings 5:1-19; Luke 4:27)

- Sends leprosy as a judgment upon Gehazi (2 Kings 5:26-27)
- Recovers the ax that had fallen into a stream (2 Kings 6:1-7)

Life Messages of Elisha

Elisha's message to those in charge was that they should turn their hearts back to God through traditional worship that honors God and acknowledges God's absolute sovereignty over every aspect of life - personal and political. When he healed the sick, it was to demonstrate God's power over life and death. When he helped in battle, it was to show God's power over nations and kingdoms.

Although Elijah was constantly in conflict with political authorities, Elisha had a much friendlier relationship with them. King Joram, the son of Ahab, was doomed by God (as prophesied by Elijah) for his corrupt leadership. Elisha later sent one of the sons of the prophets under his tutelage to authorize Jehu to kill Joram and remove Jezebel from power as prophesied by Elijah, after which Jehu was to assume the throne as the new King of Israel.

Why Did Elisha Get a Double Anointing?

Many Christians just want to add Jesus to their lives like you add a feather to a new hat. It makes them look and feel better about themselves, but doesn't do much for others. And in some cases, it helps their businesses or careers too. However, that's not the invitation that Jesus gave in the New Testament. Jesus forced people out of the Jewish Temple when they had that attitude. That's when he said, "My house shall be called a house of prayer." He also said, "Deny yourself, take up your cross and follow me." And he said, "I am the way, the truth, and the life. No man comes to the Father except through me." Doesn't it just make sense to follow the instructions that Jesus gave us? If we want to know God the Father, then we need to pay close attention to what Jesus said and do it. Don't you agree?

Four Reasons Elisha Qualified for the Double Anointing

Here are four things in 1 Kings that we need to follow if we want to receive the double anointing of God. These explain why Elisha received a double anointing.

1) **He asked for it**. God had already appointed him (1 Kings 19:16) to be Elijah's successor, but Elisha didn't just want to be head of the prophets, he wanted to maximize his effectiveness. ("Ye lust, and have not: ye kill, and desire to have, and cannot obtain: ye fight and war, yet ye have not, because ye ask not. Ye ask, and receive not, because ye ask amiss, that ye may consume *it* upon your lusts." (James 4: 3)

2) **He made it a top priority**. He left his "farming" business (1 Kings 19:19)—killing the oxen and

roasting them with the fire made from his plowing equipment. No turning back; no Plan B.

3) **He followed Elijah everywhere** he went (2 Kings 2:2-6): to Bethel (a place of worship); to Jericho (a place of obedience); and to the Jordan River (a place of dying to self; a new beginning in the spirit). We need to do all three—worship, obey, and die to our way of doing things. While there are reasons and seasons that we need to wait on God, in this situation, God is waiting on us to seek him with all of our hearts. (Matthew 6:33).

4) **He received** his new anointing by faith. Elisha's first miracle was to part the Jordan River, just as Elijah had done earlier: "Elisha picked up Elijah's cloak, which had fallen when he was taken up in the chariot. Then Elisha returned to the bank of the Jordan River. He struck the water with Elijah's cloak and cried out, "Where is the Lord, the God of Elijah?" Then the river divided, and Elisha went across." (2 Kings 2: 13-14 NLT).

While many of us today are asking, "Where is the Lord, the God of Elijah?" I believe God is asking us, "Where are the Elijahs and the Elishas that will pray and pay the price for my anointing?" The truth is IF we're willing to go through the process, God has already provided the Elisha Double Anointing (empowerment) through the cross of Jesus for whoever will believe it and take it by faith. And for those that find it and take it by faith, "the truth will set us free!"

Chapter 5: The Jesus Model of Discipleship

> **Jesus said:**
> **"Feed my sheep" and "Make disciples."**
> **We provide church members with an education in intellectual theology.**

> **(For illustrative purposes only)**
>
> **Jesus said to the well-educated rabbinical student:**
> **"Who do you say that I am?"**
>
> **The student replied:**
> **"You are the eschatological manifestation of the ground of our being - the ontological foundation of the context of our very selfhood revealed."**

One of my educational slogans is,

If education isn't practical, it's practically no good.

The American public school educational system today seems to promote a liberal arts education as a program of study that is superior to practical skills acquisition. That's one reason why America has so many looking to the government to meet their needs and to take care of them. After all, the federal government helped provide them with free K-12 education and the educational funds through FAFSA application paid for their college while also providing guaranteed educational student loans.

However, world history is strewn with the failures of autocratic, nanny governments of all kinds, including socialism, Marxism, and communism. Just as ancient Israel wanted a king to take care of them instead of God, in the same manner, many Americans today are wanting a big, nanny government to take care of them. Americans should instead turn to the God of the founding fathers – the God of American Judeo-Christian values and the Puritan ethic more commonly known as *The Bible*, The Word of God.

> **Big government can only survive with the support of small-minded people.**

No government can survive if the people it serves will not cooperate and help it succeed. So, authoritarian governments use fear and intimidation, like Jezebel and Ahab did in ancient Israel to protect their governmental power and personal interests. Like Ahab and Jezebel, American government and religious leaders want the people to serve them, rather than them serving the people. Sound familiar? From a Biblical perspective, the real battle here is a spiritual one. It's the ultimate question of who will rule in America. Will an Anti-Christ spirit of humanism, hiding behind a political ruse called the "Liberal Progressive Political Movement," continue to offer "fool's gold" to the naive? And will Americans continue to follow blindly? Or will Americans turn back to the God of Abraham, Isaac, and Jacob? Will America continue to sing another verse of the same old Blame-Game song, "It Ain't My Fault?" or will Americans take personal responsibility for our mistakes, activate 1 John 1:9 and embrace the Biblical virtues of honesty, hard work, integrity and family as we once did?

Secular Humanism is a philosophy being used by many Progressives to support the belief that humanity can solve its problems without God. They worship their gods of intellectualism, power, lust and pride. Humanism can sound logical because it's based on human reasoning and worldly wisdom. For example, I heard a young man proudly say that he was an Atheist. Then he used mathematic probabilities to reason that there must be life on other planets because there are so many universes and planets. But the same person was not willing to use his mathematical logic and his personal involvement in history to point to a Creator-God. He chose to ignore the intricacies and sophisticated physical and other scientific systems on earth and in our bodies that scream, "A God had to have done this!"

Interestingly, many college professors teach that Thomas Jefferson was a Deist - suggesting that Mr. Jefferson believed in a God that was not directly involved in human affairs. However, Mr. Jefferson encouraged the Jews, the Christians, and others to embrace their faiths and concurrent freedoms. And he supported the Declaration of Independence and the US Constitution along with the words that acknowledged a Creator (God) and certain principles that are in support of the Judeo-Christian tradition and culture. So, in my mind, the personal faith of Jefferson becomes irrelevant. The bottom line is that

Jefferson helped to create and enable laws and documents that clearly supported and encouraged people to live by the Judeo-Christian principles embraced by the American founding fathers. Both the Declaration of Independence and the US Constitution are written from a Biblical worldview, which is the exact opposite of the secular humanist principles many people are embracing today.

Can you see that a humanistic philosophy has gained prominence in American Education? This kind of educational methodology was popularized by the ancient Greeks and has been propagated by the Humanists in American Public Schools since World War II. However, they have hidden behind "Liberal Progressive Politics" **rather than acknowledge its Humanistic roots.** The Greeks believed that if a student could understand, explain and teach a particular body of information that was absent of Divine influences, then that person *was* educated. That Greek philosophy emphasized the importance of intellectual knowledge only. However, as we have already seen, the ancient Hebrew – and later the Jewish philosophy of education – stressed the role of God and obeying his words and principles.

A spiritual aspect of the Hebrew Creator-God called "Yahweh" had one additional requirement of all well-educated people: to activate the teachings of God in their daily living, while obeying God's Word, Will and Ways. The ancient Hebrew Prophets taught that it wasn't enough just to know something **intellectually**. The faithful disciple of the one true God must also learn to do/act upon the Word of God. The prophets asserted that was *real* education. The God of Abraham, Isaac and Jacob required it.

The Prophet Samuel said, "To obey is better than sacrifice, and to hearken than the fat of rams."
(1 Samuel 15:22)

And sadly, because some will be deceived into believing that intellectual assent alone is enough for them to enter the Kingdom of Heaven; they will hear the following words,

"Not everyone that saith unto me, Lord, Lord, shall enter into the kingdom of heaven; but he that doeth the will of my Father which is in heaven. Many will say to me in that day, Lord, Lord, have we not prophesied in thy name? And in thy name have cast out devils? And in thy name done many wonderful works? And then will I profess unto them, I never knew you: depart from me, ye that work iniquity."
Matthew 7:21-23 (KJV)

> **Wisdom Key:**
>
> ***"Information changes minds, but action changes lives."* (Steven K. Scott)**

The ancient Hebrews, such as the Prophet Samuel who managed a school of prophets, understood the difference between information that only affects one's *mind,* and intelligence that is activated by faith in someone's *life.*

The first time I had ever heard of "the school of the prophets" was in 2002. I was watching the Praise the Lord program on the Trinity Broadcasting Network and heard Dr. Bill Hamon, founder of *Christian International* (CI) located in Florida, share about a new apostolic-prophetic move of God. At that time, I wasn't even sure what a prophet was to be like according to the New Testament. Of course, I had been taught that there was a gift of prophecy distributed to believers as God had chosen. And because I had also been trained to be led by the Spirit of God, I found my spirit being drawn to Dr. Bill Hamon's words and mission although my Christian upbringing had included instruction that there are no more prophets, apostles or miracles today because they ceased after the apostles died. Some theologians today call that a *Cessation Doctrine or Theology.* All of this was confusing to me.

But, I knew that God's Spirit would lead me into all truth; so I continued to pray, study the Bible and listen to what the Spirit of God was teaching me. Through Dr. Bill Hamon's books, I learned about the following words of Jesus, *I didn't come into the world to do away with the law or the prophets, but to fulfill them (*Matthew 5:17*).* I also learned that the word translated as "the law" in English Bible translations more specifically meant "The Teachings of Yahweh (God)." Then I started researching other related Bible verses and discovered that there is no clear Biblical precedence for the belief that there are no more prophets, apostles or miracles today.

Because my religious leaders weren't experiencing the miracles they saw in the New Testament, they didn't see the need for apostles and prophets anymore, especially since all believers can hear God's voice and be empowered by the indwelling Spirit of God. At church, we sang songs like *"Nothing Is Impossible with God,"* while preaching that God can't or won't do certain things anymore because we're in a different "dispensation" (meaning "plan" or season) of God.

They also said that my behavior/experience should change to adapt and change to get in line with what the Bible taught, not change or adapt what the Bible taught to match my experiences. I'm sure you can see the ambiguity here. Although confusing, this was a great motivation for me to seek God with all my heart and lean not on my understanding. And like the Old Testament says, *If you seek me with all of your heart, you will surely find me* (Jeremiah 29:13). Eventually, I believe that I did find God through Christ. And of course, this book is giving me the opportunity to share some of my discoveries in the pursuit of knowing God and making him known.

Then I remembered a Bible verse that states, "*All things are possible to him who believes"* (Mark 9:23). And Jesus told his apostles (who trained 120 others): *"Greater things will you do when I go to my Father (John 14:12)."* I noticed that the Bible also said, "*God is the same yesterday, today and forever (Hebrews 13:8)"*. Considering these and other Bible verses, I didn't see any limitations placed on the followers of Jesus. And because I was determined to be a student of the Bible, not a religious denomination, I was seeking the truth from scriptures without a preconceived religious agenda.

As I continued to listen to Dr. Bill Hamon talking about training people to hear God's voice and walk in God's ways, I suddenly felt compelled to take his courses and learn from him. But there was a big problem. His school was in Florida – a long way from Grand Prairie, Texas, where I lived. So, I prayed to God and told him that I was willing to go anywhere he wanted me to go to learn whatever he wanted me to learn.

When the Student is Ready, the Teacher Always Appears.

As I began to pursue a way to learn from Dr. Hamon, I began researching his website. I noticed that his organization had regional directors in the Dallas/Fort Worth, Texas area that were close to where I lived - Mickey and Sandy Freed of Zion Ministries. After going to Mickey and Sandy's website, I noticed they offered training and mentoring under Dr. Bill Hamon's supervision and authority. I was excited! I later enrolled in all three of the courses they offered, receiving two certificates of completion: one from Dr. Bill Hamon's network called *Ministering Spiritual Gifts* and the second one from two other courses they taught that were based on several of Dr. Hamon's books.

Those classes were taught by different people in Mickey and Sandy Freed's ministry that had been trained by them. Their training turned out to be life-changing for me as I would never be the same again. I made many new Christian relationships and learned great truths as well as practical skills about how to hear God's voice and walk in his word, will and ways.

After I completed all of my formal "School of the Prophets" training and got my certificate of completion,
I agreed to serve once a month on their ministry's intercessory prayer teams. We were taught to pray for others' needs or problems, hear from God and share what we felt God said about their problems, issues or situations. Some people call that prophesying, and others call it prophetic intercession. Simply speaking, we would pray and share with them what we heard the Spirit of God saying.

The School of the Prophets Origin

The first mention of the "sons of the prophets," as all the young men educated that way were called, we find in 1 Samuel 10, when Saul is anointed as king. (1 Samuel 10:5) In the days of Samuel, there were two schools of the prophets, one in Ramah, where the prophet Samuel lived, and one in Kiryat Yearim, where the Ark of the Covenant was. Later on, some more schools of the prophets were established in Bethel (2 Kings 2:3), Jericho (2 Kings 2:15), Gilgal (2 Kings 4:38), etc.

Over time, fathers and mothers in Israel became indifferent to their obligation to God and indifferent to their responsibility to their children. Through unfaithfulness in the home, and idolatrous influences without, many of the Hebrew youth received an education differing widely from that which God had planned for them. They learned the ways of the world system.

To counter this growing evil, God (Yahweh) provided other agencies as an aid to parents in the work of education. From the earliest times, the prophets had been recognized as teachers divinely inspired and appointed. In the highest sense, the prophet was one who spoke by direct inspiration, communicating to the people the messages he/she had received from God. But the name was also given to those who, though not so directly inspired, were divinely called to instruct the people in the works and ways of God. For the training of such a class of teachers, Samuel, by the Lord's direction, established the schools of the prophets.

The Purpose of the Schools of the Prophets

The schools of the prophets were intended to serve as a barrier against the wide-spreading corruption, to provide for the mental and spiritual welfare of the youth, and to promote the prosperity of the nation by furnishing it with men qualified to act in the fear of God as leaders and advisors. To this end, Samuel gathered companies of young men who were pious, intelligent, and studious. These were called the sons of the prophets.

Elijah and Elisha were used by God in a very impressive way to stop the wave of general apostasy and to help many Israelites return to the true and only God. For several years after the call of Elisha, Elijah and Elisha labored together. Elijah had been God's instrument for the overthrowing of enormous evils. During these years of united ministry, Elijah from time to time was called upon to confront flagrant evils with a stern rebuke.

The schools of the prophets, firmly established by the Prophet Samuel, had fallen into decay during the years of Israel's apostasy. Similar to what has happened in American public schools, they quit teaching Biblical truths, forgetting that America was founded and inspired by Biblical principles. For example, the first textbooks were the Bible and Bible-based readers that used the Bible as the first and primary educational text. Those early schools in America were called "Common Schools."

In Elijah's day, we might infer that the heart of Elijah was probably encouraged as he saw what was being accomplished through these schools of the prophets. The work of reformation was not complete; but he could see throughout the kingdom a verification of the following word of the Lord spoken to Elijah,

"Yet I have left Me seven thousand in Israel, all the knees which have not bowed unto Baal." (1 Kings 19:18)

Just before Elijah was taken to heaven, he visited the schools of the prophets and instructed the students on the main points of their education. The lessons he had given them on previous visits, he now repeated, impressing upon the minds of the youth the importance of letting simplicity mark every feature of their education. Only in this way could they receive the mold of heaven, and go forth to work in the ways of the Lord. If conducted as God designs, our schools in these closing days will do work similar to that done by the schools of the prophets.

Like the Savior of humanity, of whom he was a type, Elisha in his ministry among men combined the work of healing with that of teaching. Faithfully, untiringly, throughout his long and efficient labors, Elisha endeavored to foster and advance the important educational work carried on by the schools of the prophets. In the providence of God his words of instruction to the earnest groups of young men were confirmed by the deep moving of the Spirit of God, and at times, by other unmistakable evidence of his authority as a servant of Yahweh-God.

The School of the Prophets and Their Curriculum

The primary course of study in these old Hebrew schools was the law of God (Hebrew: *Torah-teachings of Yahweh*), with the instructional emphasis given to the Law of Moses, their sacred history, sacred music, and poetry. A spirit of devotion was cherished. Not only were the students taught the duty of prayer, but they were also taught how to pray, how to approach God and have faith in Him, and how to understand and obey the teachings of his Spirit. Sanctified intellect brought forth from meditating on the Torah, and the Spirit of God was manifested in prophecy and sacred song.

The art of pure melody was diligently cultivated. No frivolous waltz was ever heard or flippant songs that would distract them and divert their attention from God; but holy, solemn psalms of praise to the Creator, exalting his name and recounting his wondrous works that reflected their ancient Biblical truths. Thus, music served a holy purpose, to lift the thoughts to that which was pure and noble and elevating, and to awaken the soul's pure devotion and gratitude toward God.

The Schools of the Prophets and Self-support

The pupils of these schools sustained themselves by their labor in tilling the soil or in some physical employment. In Israel, this was not thought strange or degrading; indeed, it was regarded as a sin to allow children to grow up in ignorance of useful labor. Every youth, whether his parents were rich or poor, was taught some trade. Even though he was to be educated for holy office, knowledge of practical life was regarded as essential to the greatest usefulness. Many of the teachers supported themselves by manual labor.

The Schools of the Prophets and Teacher Qualifications

The instructors were well versed in divine truth, but had enjoyed communion with God, and had received the special endowment of his Spirit. They had the respect and confidence of the people, both for learning and for good character and morals.

The 400 Silent Years

There were 400 years of silence during the time between the Old Testament and New Testament, during which God did not speak to the Jewish people. The 400 years of silence began with the warning that closed the Old Testament: "*Behold, I am going to send you Elijah the prophet before the coming of the great and terrible day of the LORD. He will restore the hearts of the fathers to their children and the hearts of the children to their fathers so that I will not come and smite the land with a curse*" (Malachi 4:5-6) and ended with the coming of John the Baptist, the Messiah's forerunner.

At the time of Malachi's warning, about 430 BC, the Jews had returned to Palestine from the Babylonian captivity (as merchants, not shepherds). The Medo-Persian Empire still ruled Palestine, and the Temple had been rebuilt. Both the Law and the priesthood of Aaron's line had been restored, and the Jews had given up their worship of idols. Nevertheless, Malachi's warning was not without cause. The Jewish people were mistreating their wives, marrying pagans, and not tithing. The priests were neglecting the temple and not teaching the people the ways of God. In short, the Jews were not honoring God.

In 333 BC, Palestine fell to the Greeks, and in 323 BC it fell to the Egyptians. The Jews were treated well throughout those reigns, and they adopted the Greek language, as well as many of the Greek customs and manners. In Egypt, the Old Testament was translated into Greek. That translation, the Septuagint, came into widespread use (and is frequently quoted in the New Testament).

Jewish law and the priesthood remained more or less intact until Antiochus the Great of Syria captured Palestine in 204 BC. He and his successor, Antiochus Epiphanes, persecuted the Jews and sold the priesthood in 171 BC. Epiphanes desecrated the Holy of Holies. This desecration resulted in an uprising by Judas Maccabeus of the priestly line of Aaron, and in 165 BC the Jews recaptured Jerusalem and cleansed the temple. However, fighting continued between the Jews and the Syrians until the Romans gained control of Palestine in 63 BC, at which time Pompey walked into the Holy of Holies, once again shocking and embittering the Jews. In 47 BC, Caesar installed Antipater, a descendant of Esau, as procurator of Judea, and Antipater subsequently appointed his two sons as kings of Galilee and Judea.

As the New Testament opens, Antipater's son, Herod the Great, (a descendant of Esau and not of the line of Aaron) was king, and the priesthood was politically motivated. Politics also resulted in the development of two major factions, the Sadducees, and the Pharisees.

The Sadducees favored the liberal attitudes and practices of the Greeks. They only practiced the laws of the Torah in their religious activities, but like all aristocrats in that time, they didn't believe God should have an active influence in their nonreligious activities. It was the initial separation of church and state doctrine that was the separation of personal faith and the state, similar to the popular and politically correct belief in American politics.

The American doctrine of separation of church and state has evolved into the separation of personal faith and the state.

The Pharisees were conservative zealots who, with the help of the scribes, developed a religious law to the point where the concerns and cares of the people were virtually meaningless. Additionally, synagogues, new places of worship and social activity, had sprouted up all over the country. Religious and civil matters were governed by the lesser and the greater Sanhedrin.

A chief priest and seventy other members made up the Sanhedrin that handed out justice, sometimes as severe as 39 lashes administered with full force.

Between the time of Malachi and the coming of the Messiah, several prophecies were fulfilled, including the 2,300 days of desecration between 171 and 165 BC (Daniel 8:14). Neither the fulfilled prophecies nor the 400 years the nation was given to study Scripture, to seek God (Psalm 43-44) and to prepare for the coming Messiah, was put to good use. In fact, those years blinded and deafened the nation to the point where most of the Jews could not even consider the concept of a humble Messiah (Zechariah 9:9; Isaiah 6:10; John 12:40).

Almost two millennia have passed since the New Testament canon was completed, and though the Word is full of grace and truth, and though the birth, life, and death of Jesus fulfilled a staggering array of prophecies, the Jews as a people have yet to open their eyes and ears. But Jesus is coming again, and one day a remnant will both see and hear.

The Schools of the Prophets in the Time of Jesus

After the 400 years of silence, there were no real schools of the prophets anymore. In the first century, the education the young people received was not like the one from the old schools of the prophets, moving away from their prophetic roots and becoming more secular. They began to change from the schools of the prophets to the schools of liberal arts education like America has done. However, they did have religious schools, organized around all the synagogues and the Temple. In many ways, these were the equivalent of modern Christian schools. The Jews considered them schools of the prophets. In name, the schools seemed to be the same, but the content and methodology of education were very different.

I have found no evidence that Jesus' disciples studied in those schools. Seven of the twelve apostles were humble fishermen. They were poor in worldly goods, but rich in the knowledge and practice of the truth, which in the sight of Heaven, gave them the highest ranking as teachers. They had not been students in the schools of the prophets, but for three years they had been taught by the greatest Teacher the world has ever known – Jesus. Under his instruction, they had become elevated, intelligent, and refined agents through whom men might be led to the knowledge of the truth.

Jesus was never sent to any of the Jewish religious schools during his time. And this was not because

Mary and Joseph were exclusivists, but most likely because the education you could receive in those times from the established schools didn't follow God's plan. John the Baptist's parents were led by the Holy Spirit to make the same choice for the education of their son for some of the same reasons. Their example is inspirational for our times: when the current schools don't follow God's plan for education, the healthiest choice is to home school your children.

The phrase "school of the prophets" is first mentioned in the Old Testament with the prophet Samuel and the group of prophets he trained. The phrase describes the company of prophets that came forth as an instrument of God's authority, speaking his Word and creating his will in the earth. Samuel's school of the prophets set people free from spiritual oppression, protected God's leaders from harm, and aided Israel in honoring God's Word, Will and Ways.

Within a school of the prophets, spiritual powers and abilities (also called *anointings*) were transferred from one individual to another through training, prayer, and mentorship. The prophet Elisha is a great example of this. His "credentials" were simply that he was the servant and mentor of Elijah. Elisha became a mighty prophet because he was taught particular spiritual truths as he served Elijah, and he received a double portion of Elijah's anointing. In this case, it seems that some things are better caught than just taught. The training of the young prophets occurred the same way as Jesus trained the 12 Apostles and they trained others to do the same. I will share more about this later in this next.

The Jesus Model of Discipleship

Let's look at the Jesus Model of Discipleship. Of course, you could also call it, *The Biblical Model of Discipleship*. This model was very simple. They educated, demonstrated and activated their students in the teachings of Yahweh (God) like a father to his sons.

The Old Testament first mentions a school of prophets in **1 Samuel 19:18–24** and in **2 Kings 2 and 4:38–44** (some translations say "company of prophets" or "sons of the prophets"). Also, the prophet Amos possibly infers a prophetic school in stating his credentials (or lack thereof) to King Amaziah: "I was neither a prophet nor the son of a prophet" (Amos 7:14).

First Samuel 19 relates an account in which King Saul sends messengers to arrest David. When these men encountered a company of prophets under Samuel's leadership, the king's men also prophesied. This happened three times. Saul himself then went, and he too foretold the future, leading people to ask, "Is Saul also among the prophets?" (1 Samuel 19:24), which became a saying in those days.

The company of prophets was probably comprised of Levites who served in roles related to the tabernacle and ceremonial worship. The content of their "prophecies" is not specified. Their messages could have been general teachings from God's teachings in the Books of Moses, or they could have included additional revelation.

In 2 Kings 2, Elijah was traveling with Elisha, and a group of prophets from Bethel told Elisha that Elijah would be taken from him that day (verse 3). Another group of prophets at Jericho repeated the prophecy (verse 5), and the third group of prophets near the Jordan River delivered the same message (verse 7). The third group of 50 men may have been a subset of the gathering of prophets at Jericho. After Elijah was taken up into heaven, Elisha reluctantly sent 50 of these prophets to search for Elijah for three days as read in verses 15-18.

In 2 Kings 4:38-41 Elisha was in Gilgal during a time of famine. Elisha miraculously changed an inedible "stew" into an edible dish for the group of prophets there. Chapter 4 ends with Elisha's turning 20 loaves of bread into more than enough food for 100 people. Nothing else is mentioned about this school of prophets, although it is clear that they lived together in some community and were known as the sons of the prophets who worshiped the Lord. The words "sons of the prophets" was indicative of the close and transparent relationships that God taught to the ancient Hebrews through his prophets. The phrase also suggests a 24/7 training relationship like a father and son could have.

These groups of men are believed to be some of the leaders among the 7,000 Israelites who did not bow down to Baal, as God told Elijah in 1 Kings 19:18. There were at least three schools or communities of these prophets and possibly more, consisting of men who were devoted to God and served him. They followed the teachings of Moses, Samuel, Elijah and Elisha and were widely known as "the sons of the prophets."

What Is the Jesus Model of Discipleship?

I call the Jesus Model of Discipleship "the lost art of mentorship," because very few seem to understand it today; and the church has not corporately emphasized it since about the third century AD. Oh, there have been times that some have attempted to disciple other people, but most of them have crashed and burned, perhaps because it wasn't just like Jesus did it.

I rarely use the word "discipleship" anymore because of the preconceived ideas many have when they see or hear the word "discipleship." One such example was in the 1980's. It was called the "Discipleship Movement." But, unfortunately, this movement began to emphasize physical "dos and don'ts" while de-emphasizing the importance of the Holy Spirit individually speaking and guiding the trainer and the trainee. In other words, their form of discipleship was more about "controlling" the outward behaviors of those being trained, than about teaching them how to feed themselves with the Word of God, while listening and obeying the Spirit of God.

According to Jesus, he didn't come to be served, but to serve. How many times have I seen pastors and other church leaders with a different paradigm! They think that their members should serve their vision and their way of doing things, rather than serve the Kingdom of God. And God forbid if someone dares to disagree with the Pastor! The Bible gives clear instructions about how to deal with disagreements in the church. And for purposes here, I'll just mention what the Bible says about church leaders in Matthew 20: 25-28, *"Jesus called them together and said, 'You know that the rulers of the Gentiles lord it over them, and their high officials exercise authority over them. Not so with you. Instead, whoever wants to become great among you must be your servant, and whoever wants to be first must be your slave— just as the Son of Man did not come to be served, but to serve, and to give his life as a ransom for many.'"*

I believe this kind of religion is frequently narcissistic and entirely of human origin! I've lost count of the times I have observed various denominations that have caused their members to feel guilty or shameful because they didn't support a specific activity. I don't believe that this kind of "leadership" is from God.

> **Wisdom Key:**
> **We need to learn to pray in agreement with specific Bible verses and not just vent our feelings, while trying to beg God to do something.**

There have been limited moments in church history when the church has practiced biblical discipleship. And as a result, those churches, countries, cities and cultures were totally transformed, while experiencing unparalleled prosperity and soaring increases in church attendance. We need to learn how Jesus equipped and trained the twelve Apostles and replicate them. That is what this book is about – opening Christians' eyes to the need and method of biblical discipleship. Or as some have said, learn to "DWJD" - do what Jesus did.

In modern days, most churches have been spending 90% of their time and money teaching and training the 10% (or less) of Christians who are clergy (full-time vocational ministers), and they have completely forgotten how to disciple their "lay church members" in successful marketplace ministries. Many American churches are primarily building a religious institution, while Christ is all about building his Kingdom. And since Jesus said, "...if I be lifted up, I will draw all men unto me" (John 12:32) and that he would *build his church* and the gates of Hell would not prevail against it (Matthew 16:18), why are so many ministers trying to build their churches and their kingdoms *their* way?

A good example of this mistake is found in the story of David, son of Jesse, and King Saul. The Prophet Samuel persistently took God's Word to Saul, but he lived his way and did things in his timing.

> **It has been an enlightening experience for me to read the story of David in 1 and 2 Samuel. I simply imagined that King Saul represented some full-time ministers of various denominations in America and David represented the ministers that are all about the Kingdom of God and his way of doing and being (Matthew 6:33).**

In America, we have thousands of 'denominations' – another word for *kingdom* - another word for *government*. Simply put, the word "kingdom" simply means the domain (government) of a king or ruler. Like with a kingdom, many religious denominations have a fiduciary (formal/legal) obligation through the governing board of their denomination to build and establish their kind of religious dominion (government) to the exclusion of all others. I think that this is too frequently about building their denominational kingdom and not about building the Kingdom of God.

The evidence of this is revealed by the "fruit" of that church or organization. In the book of Galatians, we learn that love must be the motive of good church government – love for God and each other, yielding the fruit of the Spirit. How many churches make you feel loved when you attend them? And how many sermons have you heard that criticized people, rather than offering the wisdom of God to its listeners, realizing that if the Lord doesn't build the church, it will be constructed in vain (Psalm 127: 1)?

Let's review some "church building basics", according to Jesus. The church of Jesus Christ is not a pastor's church or a denomination's church. It's the Lord's church. Secondly, no man or woman can build the church of Christ, because Jesus said that it is his church and that he would build it. How? Jesus said that if we lift him up, he will build his church by drawing all men to himself. And the method that he implemented was discipleship - not seminars, church teachings, retreats or other religious programs, although all of these can be a great support to successfully disciple others.

In the English language, we've historically described the mentoring process with words like *"disciple,"* *"coach,"* and *"apprentice."* The word *disciple* is usually used for religious training; the word *coach* is mostly used for athletic training, and the word *apprentice* is used for workforce training for trades such as electricians and carpenters.

The term "biblical discipleship" here is not referring to another human-made church program, but to the effective leadership model of Jesus and his disciples. In the New Testament, Paul first wrote that John Mark was not beneficial to him in the ministry but later – after John Mark received additional discipleship from Barnabas – Paul wrote that John Mark *was* beneficial to him in the ministry.

Barnabas mentored Paul and John Mark, while Paul mentored John Mark. Their effective implementation of Biblical discipleship was evidenced by the change in Paul's eventual acceptance of John Mark for ministry. It's also one of the main reasons they were sent out in pairs – one master (experienced) trainer and one apprentice (beginner) trainee.

The biblical training model was not programmatic, but it was symptomatic of their understanding of the Great Commission. Matthew 28:19 says, "Go therefore and make disciples of all the nations, baptizing them (teach, train and activate them), teaching them to observe all things that I have commanded you" (train them to experience all of the same things you have experienced). That's why Jesus said, "Follow me," rather than simply, "Teach what I teach." The Apostle Paul confirmed this when he wrote; "Follow me as I follow Christ."

Discipleship is a relationship, requiring uncommon involvement, commitment, responsibility and accountability for the mentor and the one being mentored. Even the word "Christian" infers the same message, because it means "one who follows after the anointed one and his anointing (Christ)."

Use the Force, Luke!

I believe one of the best modern models of biblical discipleship was the depiction of the Jedi Knight training in the Star Wars movies. The Jedi Council could represent the leaders of a local church, which was made up of Jedi Knight Masters. The Jedi Knight

Masters were granted one person as their apprentice.

In the Star War movies, each Jedi Knight Master depended on his apprentice to serve his common cause, to learn to "use the force" and to be willing to submit to the Jedi Master's leadership. Then when the apprentice was ready to be released, the Jedi Master, in cooperation with the Jedi Council, promoted the apprentice to a Jedi Master; after which, he would patiently wait for a new apprentice to be assigned.

Considering the ways of Jesus, we will notice that He taught (illustrated truths), trained (demonstrated truths) and activated those truths (now you do it). Today, these are the same three steps used in apprenticeship programs that help prepare workers to be successful in various vocational trades such as electricians and carpenters.

In James 1: 22-24, the Bible says, *"Be ye doers of the word, and not hearers only, deceiving yourselves. For if anyone is a hearer of the word and not a doer, he is like a man observing his natural face in a mirror; for he observes himself, goes away, and immediately forgets what kind of man he was"*.

And in James 2: 20, James wrote: *"...faith without works is dead."*

Therefore, we can conclude that Jesus did not just teach truths, but he also trained and activated all of those who were willing to follow him and become his disciples. Today, however, few want to invest the time and personal commitment to follow Christ, because that requires them to "deny themselves and take up their crosses..."(Matthew 16:24). True discipleship requires learning how to overcome "the deceitfulness of riches" about which Jesus warned in his parables such as the one in Matthew 13:22.

> **Words of Wisdom**
> **Some teach, but don't train or activate, while others teach and train, but don't activate; others just train and activate, but don't teach. However, Jesus did all three: he taught, demonstrated and activated.**

It's enlightening to consider that Jesus was a carpenter and a family businessman before he became the Savior and the Messiah. For about 30 years, Jesus was taught, trained and activated (mentored) as a successful carpenter and businessman with no known formal ministry. These are the same fundamental skills that Jesus later used to disciple the 12 Apostles, and that the 12 Apostles, in turn, implemented to mentor many others. For example, in Luke 10, Jesus sent out seventy ministers who enthusiastically returned to him after discovering that they could do some of the same things they saw Jesus and the apostles do such as cast out devils. But in verse 20 Jesus said, "...nevertheless do not rejoice in this, that the spirits are subject to you, but rather rejoice because your names are written in heaven." Why? I believe one reason is that Jesus wanted them to understand and remember that the depth of their character was far more important than the signs, wonders, and miracles that followed them. In other words, God created us to take dominion over things and love people - NOT to take dominion over people and love things.

> **God created humankind to take dominion over things and love people – NOT to take dominion over people and love things.**

As the result of this kind of discipleship, a little less than three hundred years later, the Roman Emperor Constantine reportedly became a Christian and made Christianity the state religion of Rome. The Roman Empire changed from slaughtering and persecuting

Christians to embracing them and their faith in Christ! However, it seems in just 200 years or less, they stopped practicing the art of discipleship, as evidenced by the educational roles allowed non-believing Greeks, like Plato, Aristotle, and Socrates whom they allowed to teach their children.

As a result, they inadvertently birthed the Holy Roman Empire and the Roman Catholic Church, while changing Christianity from a distinctly Hebrew and Jewish worship of God to a new, Romanized version that suited Constantine. The word "catholic" literally means "universal"; thus, for about one thousand years (500 AD-1500 AD), it became the only recognized Universal Christian Church until the Protestant Reformation in the 1500's. Today, our US History books call this period "The Dark Ages" or "The Middle Ages."

This biblical model of discipleship is about multiplying. It's about "Go Ye" into all of the world, not "Come Ye" into all of our religious institutions. Let's look at the math of the Kingdom of God.

1 +1 = 2 (Jesus and his first disciple)
2 + 2 = 4 (Jesus and his first disciple train one other person each)

$$4 + 4 = 8 \text{ (Repeat)}$$
$$8 + 8 = 16 \text{ (Repeat)}$$
$$16 + 16 = 32$$
$$32 + 32 = 64$$
$$64 + 64 = 128$$
$$128 + 128 = 256$$
$$256 + 256 = 512$$
$$512 + 512 = 1,024$$
$$1024 + 1024 = 2,048$$
$$2,048 + 2,048 = 4,096$$
$$4,096 + 4,096 = 8192$$
$$8,192 + 8,192 = 16,384$$
$$16,384 + 16,384 = 32,768$$
$$32,768 + 32,768 = 65,536$$
$$65,536 + 65,536 = 131,072$$
$$131,072 + 131,072 = 262,144$$

I think you get the idea. Now *that* is exciting! Perhaps that was what God meant when he inspired Adam and Eve in Genesis to *take dominion, be fruitful and MULTIPLY!*

Chapter 6: God's Word, Will, and Ways

Before Jehu could assume the throne as the new King of Israel, he was instructed to "clean house." It was probably something like the "cleaning" that took place in Hebrew homes at the time of the Passover and especially the "Feast of Unleavened Bread" (Exodus 12:16-20; 13:5-1). The feasts were the times when the house would be cleaned and a search would be made for the presence of any leaven, which would be removed when found.

Jehu was told by God to clean the house (dynasty) of Omri and to purge Ahab (Omri's son) from Israel. The house of Omri had been a leavening agent in the northern kingdom of Israel for too long, and the time had finally come to "clean up." In this regard, Jehu will do a thorough job with only one exception: Jehu does not rid the nation of all false worship. Nevertheless, Jehu's rise to power is a day of reckoning for those who have played a part in promoting evil in the land of Israel.

Jehu is named in 1 Kings 19:16-17; but he does not appear until 2 Kings 9. The story of Jehu's "house cleaning" begins long before 2 Kings 9. In a way, it starts with Omri, who was popularly recognized as Israel's king rather than Zimri. Zimri was a commander in the army of Israel who killed Elah, then king of Israel, and reigned in his place for a week.

The military preferred Omri, who eventually emerged as the head of a new dynasty, since Zimri had killed Elah and all his heirs. Thus, Baasha's dynasty ended; (see 1 Kings 15:27–16:7). When Omri died, his son Ahab took the throne of the northern kingdom of Israel. Ahab and his wife Jezebel dominated the scene since 1 Kings 16. The last member of the dynasty of Omri was Joram (also known as Jehoram), the son of Ahab. He took the throne after the death of his brother, Ahaziah.

The sins of Ahab and Jezebel, compounded with the sins of Ahaziah and his brother Joram, provoked divine condemnation, resulting in the prophecy that the house of Omri would perish. The first prophecy of these matters comes in 1 Kings 19:15-18 followed by other reinforcing prophesies (1 Kings 20:41-43; 21:20-29; 22:17-23). Ahab's death took place before that of his wife, Jezebel, and is considerably more honorable (1 Kings 22) than hers due to Ahab's repentance (1 Kings 21:27-29).
But now the time has finally come for judgment to fall on the house of Omri, and his son, Ahab. Elisha

sends a son of the prophets to Ramoth Gilead to anoint Jehu as king over Israel. He is very clearly instructed to strike the house of Ahab and to kill every male member of his family as a judgment against him for shedding the blood of his servants and prophets. It is also made clear that Jezebel will die and that the dogs will devour her body (2 Kings 9:6-10).

When his fellow commanders pledge their support to Jehu as their new king, he sets out for Jezreel, where Israel's King Joram (son of the deceased Ahab), Judah's King Ahaziah, and Jezebel (Joram's mother, and Ahab's widow) are staying. As Jehu races toward Jezreel, both Joram and Ahaziah go outside the city of Jezreel to meet him, not suspecting that a revolution is in progress. Providentially, they meet at the property that belonged to Naboth. Joram seeks to flee, as does Ahaziah, but both are executed. Jehu then marches upon the city of Jezreel where he instructs those standing near Jezebel to throw her out of the window from which she was taunting him.

Jezebel probably died as the result of her fall, but being trampled under the feet of Jehu's horses (and perhaps also being run over by his chariot) certainly ended not only her life, but a reign of wickedness.

When the dogs devoured most all of her remains, the prophecies about her death were fulfilled.

But there was still much to do to consolidate Jehu's rule. There remained many who had done evil and they were to be punished Additionally, there were many who would pose a constant threat to Jehu's reign as king over Israel, including the heirs of Ahab, the sons of Joram.

Second Kings 10 describes the way in which Jehu eliminated all of the remaining heirs and political allies of Joram and some of those who supported Ahaziah. While his campaign is a violent one, it is exceedingly skillful and precise, as I will attempt to communicate. So, let's continue then to the events of 2 Kings 10 and to the description of Jehu's consolidation of his kingdom.

Destroying an Evil Dynasty
(2 Kings 10:1-11)

The House of Ahab had 70 sons living in Samaria. So Jehu wrote letters and sent them to Samaria to the leading officials of Jezreel and the guardians of Ahab's dynasty. This is what the letter said,

"You have with you the sons of your master, chariots and horses, a fortified city, and weapons. So when this letter arrives, pick the best and most capable of your master's sons, place him on his father's throne, and defend your master's dynasty."

Those who received the letter were terrified and said, "Look, two kings could not stop him! How can we?" So the palace supervisor, the city commissioner, the leaders, and guardians sent this message to Jehu, "We are your subjects. Whatever you say, we will do. We will not make anyone king. Do what you consider proper."

Jehu then wrote them a second letter saying,

"If you are really on my side and willing to obey me, then take the heads of your master's sons and come to me in Jezreel at this time tomorrow."

Keep in mind that the king (Joram) had 70 male children, and the prominent men of the city were raising them. When they received the letter, they seized the king's sons and executed all 70 of them. They put their heads in baskets and sent them to Jehu in Jezreel. The messenger came and told Jehu, "They have brought the heads of the king's sons."

Jehu said, "Stack them in two piles at the entrance of the gate until morning."

The following morning, Jehu went out and stood there. Then he said to all the people, "You are innocent. I conspired against my master and killed him. But who struck down all of these men? Therefore, take note that not one of the judgments the LORD announced against Ahab's dynasty has failed to materialize. The LORD had done what he announced through his servant Elijah."

Then Jehu killed all who were left of Ahab's family in Jezreel, and all his nobles, close friends, and priests. He left no survivors.

In some forms of athletic competition, the scoring is based upon the "level of difficulty." If an ice skater beautifully performs a single rotation, no one is impressed, and their score will be low. It was easy to do—too easy. But if one were to perform a triple rotation beautifully, the score would be high because it is tough to perform this feat. As we approach the conclusion of the story of Jehu's rise to power, we will reflect on the level of difficulty of his accomplishments.

Consider these factors:

It is one thing to march on a city and wipe out everyone, as Ben Hadad or Hazael sought to do. It is quite another to selectively eliminate individuals without harming others.

1) Jehu is caught completely off-guard by the arrival of the prophet and by the news that he is to become the next king of Israel, in place of Ahab and Jezebel's son, Joram. Perhaps unlike Hazael, Jehu had not entertained the thought of overthrowing Joram. If one is to succeed at a military coup, months of planning and preparation are required. There was obviously none of this, as the account in chapter 9 reveals. Jehu was propelled into his role; he was forced to act quickly and without any careful preparation.

2) Jehu had been given a clear mandate about his mission and what he was to accomplish. He was to become the king of Israel. He was instructed to execute those responsible for promoting evil in the land, and/or who would resist a change of power and thus pose a threat to his kingdom. His 166 victims were confirmed by the Prophet(s), and were few.

3) One of Jehu's primary tasks was to locate and to execute every heir of Joram (the House of Ahab), a task Joram had made sure would be almost impossible to accomplish. First, he had placed his sons in Samaria, the capital city of Israel, and the most well-fortified and ably defended city in the nation. Furthermore, he had 70 sons who were dispersed about the city. Joram had placed his sons in the homes of various dignitaries. Jehu would not be able to storm the capital and somehow isolate all of Joram's sons in a single location. How would Jehu know how many sons there were, where they could be found (exactly), and how to identify them? The elimination of Joram's sons looked like an impossible mission.

4) Jehu was in Jezreel, some 25 miles or so from Samaria. Taking control of Jezreel was a beginning, but it was certainly not the most difficult task facing Jehu. His work was cut out for him.

5) Jehu's strength was not as pronounced as we might suppose. So far as we have been

informed in 2 Kings 9, Jehu has killed only three people: Joram, Ahaziah, and Jezebel.

I do not think the size of Jehu's "army" was very significant at that moment either. You will recall that Jehu was but one of the commanders in Ramoth Gilead. "All Israel," was there defending the city against an attack by Hazael of Syria (2 Kings 9:14). Most of the Israelite soldiers had to remain in Ramoth Gilead to protect this vital outpost. When Jehu left the city, he instructed his fellow-commanders to blockade it, so that no one could get to Jezreel before him with news of the revolt. This indicates that most of the soldiers were staying behind. We are not told of a large army leaving with Jehu and indeed this would not have been possible.

Additionally, a large army would only have hindered Jehu at that moment. He is racing (driving furiously—9:20) to Jezreel in his chariot, and thus anyone accompanying him would have to be on horseback or in a chariot as well. There is no slow-marching army with Jehu, and thus his soldiers are "a few good men."

Military Genius or the Hand of God?

Perhaps if the people of the city of Samaria had known the small size and strength of Jehu's forces, they might have opposed him rather than surrendering. What we see in chapters 9 and 10 then is nothing short of a miracle!

When Jehu is anointed as king of Israel, he is told that he must totally wipe out all of the male descendants of Ahab's son, Joram. The evil dynasty of Omri is to be terminated. At that time, Jehu is still in Jezreel, the vacation palace of Ahab, now belonging to Ahab's son Joram. It seems to be the dwelling place of Joram's mother, Jezebel, as well.

The capital of the northern kingdom of Israel is Samaria. Joram has 70 sons who are potential heirs to his throne, and all of these sons live in Samaria or the vicinity, cared for by various members of the nobility that live there.

How was Jehu going to seize control of Samaria with all of its defenses when he had so few men with him? And how was he to identify and eliminate Joram's sons when the nobility of Samaria was charged with keeping them, and when they most certainly would not be disposed to handing them over to Jehu for execution? What could Jehu possibly do to accomplish the mission God had given to him?

Jehu's approach portrays a real genius. He does not march on Samaria with his handful of a "few good men." Had the people of Samaria seen the size of Jehu's "army," they would most certainly have chosen to fight. They might even have laughed. Jehu made an incredibly bold move.

Jehu sends a messenger to Samaria with letters addressed to the leaders of the city, challenging them to fight. He does not make any claims or boasts; he reminds them of their assets. They have the heirs to the throne in their city. They are within fortified walls, and they have the chariots and the weapons with which to fight. In effect, Jehu has given them every good reason to fight him. And so he issues the challenge: Let them choose which heir will be their next king, and then let them fight.

If the leaders of Samaria knew what we know, they might have fought. It would appear that they could hardly have lost (apart from divine intervention). Instead, the leaders of the city chose to unconditionally surrender to Jehu. But why did they yield when they had all the advantages—advantages that Jehu called to their attention? I believe our text tells us why. They had never seen Jehu's "army," but they had heard reports—perhaps I should say they had heard *rumors*. They knew Jehu had somehow managed to kill both the King of Israel and the King of Judah. They apparently did not know how this had happened, and so they allowed their imaginations to run away with them.

They assumed that the only way Jehu could have killed these two kings is by overpowering them, by his army outnumbering their armies. If this were true, then Jehu must have had a massive army and that army could surely lay siege to Samaria, or even break down its walls.

Jehu appears to have bluffed, and it worked. Word of their surrender reaches Jezreel. They would do whatever Jehu asked. However, Jehu still does not leave Jezreel to march on Samaria. If they were to see the little size of his "army," they might change their minds and fight.

And so Jehu makes yet another bold move. He sends another message to the leaders of Samaria in response to their unconditional surrender. Jehu reminds them that they said they would do whatever he commanded; then, with that in mind, Jehu orders them to execute the sons of the king, who would be heirs to the throne.

So far as our text tells us, Jehu never mentioned how many sons there were. Perhaps he did not even know at this moment in time, but he did not let them know that. And, so that there would be proof and verification of their compliance with his demands, Jehu ordered them to place the heads of these sons in baskets and deliver them to him at Jezreel within 24 hours.

Jehu does not give the leaders of Samaria time to ponder their decision or to take counter measures. By his deadline, he forces them to act immediately. Jezreel is approximately 25 miles away from Samaria. These messengers will have to hurry to get back to Samaria, deliver Jehu's mandate, put the sons of the king to death, and then return to Jezreel with their heads, all within 24 hours. They must either carry out Jehu's command promptly or fight—and they have already decided not to resist. In haste, the king's sons are put to death, and their heads are taken to the entrance of the gate of Jezreel.

Jehu has done a fantastic job of maintaining control of this situation. He has used their fear, and he has managed to prevent any outsider from entering the city gates of Jezreel, where they would be able to observe the size of Jehu's forces. The Samaritan leaders are intimidated by what they believe Jehu's army to be, and they are entirely deceived as to his real strength. It is his cunning that wins this war, not his strength.

The Original Talking Heads

Seventy heads are placed in two piles, just outside the city gates of Jezreel, and they are left there overnight. Does this allow Jehu to inspect these heads in the cover of darkness to verify that his orders have been obeyed? It almost seems so. In the morning, Jehu walks outside of the gate. I would imagine that he stations himself midway between the two piles of heads so that his words would be dramatically underscored.

I believe that he is speaking primarily to the people of Jezreel (no more than a few men would have been required to deliver the heads and they could have already left to return to Samaria.) He tells them that so far as the execution of Joram is concerned, he alone bears the responsibility. But when it comes to the death of those whose heads are now before them all, Jehu asks them to consider who bears liability for them. In a technical sense, Jehu is responsible for this also, since he issued the order to kill the sons of Joram. But the leaders of Samaria carried out the actual killing. And, in some sense, the people of Jezreel have become participants in this revolution as well by the fact that they are there.

In other words, Jehu leads them to understand that they are all in this together. This is another turning point in the revolution. There is no turning back. Joram and every one of his heirs is dead.

Jehu had killed the king and ordered the execution of Joram's sons, but the people participated, and there is no way of turning back the clock. The deed is done, and they have had a hand in it. There is no other way for them to go but to follow Jehu. The final argument that Jehu offers is his reminder that all of these things have happened at the command of God. These things are what God had indicated through his prophet, Elijah. God's will had been done.

The people of Jezreel find Jehu's arguments compelling, and thus it is at this point that Jehu kills all those in Jezreel who are relatives of Ahab, as well as his loyal supporters, even including the priests (verse 11). Lest we question this and suggest (as some have done) that Jehu has gone too far here, let me remind you that at least some of these were participants in the mockery of justice which resulted in the death of Naboth and his sons, and the theft of his property by Jezebel and Ahab. Let's read the account from God's Word:

His wife Jezebel said to him, "You are the king of Israel! Get up, eat some food and have a real time. I will get the vineyard of Naboth the Jezreelite for you."

She wrote out orders, signed Ahab's name to them, and sealed them with his seal. She then sent the orders to the leaders and to the nobles who lived in Naboth's city. This is what she wrote: "Observe a time of fasting and seat Naboth in front of the people. Also, seat two villains opposite him and have them testify, 'You cursed God and the king.' Then take him out and stone him to death."' The men of the city, the leaders and the nobles who lived there, followed the written orders Jezebel had sent them. They observed a time of fasting and put Naboth in front of the people. The two villains arrived and sat opposite. Then the villains testified against Naboth right before the people, saying, "Naboth cursed God and the king." So they led him outside the city and stoned him to death. Then they reported to Jezebel, "Naboth has been stoned to death" (1 Kings 21:7-14, emphasis mine).

We must certainly see that in order to gain and maintain their positions, the nobility of Jezreel participated in many of the wicked schemes of Ahab, Joram, and Jezebel. They were not innocent bystanders. And they were the very ones who could also orchestrate the downfall of Jehu. The priests, likewise, were a part of Joram's corrupt administration. Jehu was "cleaning house" and this surely needed to be done. Jehu's claim that these things were the fulfillment of God's judgment upon this dynasty, and upon these people is quite evident.

Jehu's Journey to Samaria
(2 Kings 10:12-28)

Jehu then left there and set out for Samaria. While he was traveling through Beth Eked of the Shepherds, Jehu ran into the relatives of Ahaziah king of Judah. He asked, "Who are you?" They replied, "We are Ahaziah's relatives. We have come down to see how the king's sons and the queen mother's sons are doing." He said, "Capture them alive!" So they captured them alive and then executed all 42 of them in the cistern at Beth Eked; he left no survivors. When he left there, he met Jehonadab, son of Rekab, who had been looking for him. Jehu greeted him and asked, "Are you as committed to me as I am to you?" Jehonadab answered, "I am!" Jehu replied, "If so, give me your hand." So he offered his hand, and Jehu pulled him up into the chariot. Jehu said, "Come with me and see how zealous I am for the LORD's cause." So he took him along in his chariot. He went to Samaria and exterminated all the members of Ahab's family who were still alive in Samaria, just as the LORD had announced to Elijah. Jehu assembled all the people and said to them, "Ahab worshiped Baal a little; Jehu will worship him with great devotion. So now, bring to me all the prophets of Baal, as well as all his servants and priests. None of them must be absent, for I am offering a great sacrifice to Baal. Any of them who fail to appear will lose their lives."

But Jehu was tricking them so he could destroy the servants of Baal. Then Jehu ordered, "Make arrangements for a celebration for Baal." So they announced it. Jehu sent invitations throughout Israel, and all the servants of Baal came; not one was absent. They arrived at the temple of Baal and filled it up from end to end. Jehu ordered the one *who was in charge of the wardrobe, "Bring out robes for all the servants of Baal." So he brought out robes for them. Then Jehu and Jehonadab son of Rekab went to the temple of Baal. Jehu said to the servants of Baal, "Make sure there are no servants of the LORD here with you; there must be only servants of Baal."*

They went inside to offer sacrifices and burnt sacrifices. Now Jehu had stationed 80 men outside. He had told them, "If any of the men inside get away, you will pay with your lives." When he finished offering the burnt sacrifice, Jehu ordered the royal guard and officers, "Come in and strike them down! Don't let any escape!" So the royal guard and officers struck them down with the sword and left their bodies lying there. Then they entered the inner sanctuary of the temple of Baal. They hauled out the sacred pillar of Baal and burned it. They demolished the sacred pillar of Baal and the temple of Baal; it is used as a latrine to this very day. So Jehu eradicated Baal worship from Israel.

The more I read this account, the more amazed I am at the ways in which God providentially placed his enemies in the hands of Jehu and his men. The things that Jehu had been able to accomplish were amazing, but it was not until after the nobility of Samaria had executed the 70 sons of the king that Jehu approached the city. On his way to Samaria, Jehu happened upon a group of 42 people who were on their way to Jezreel. These were relatives of Ahaziah, the wicked king of Judah, whom Jehu had recently put to death. They were unaware of the events that had just taken place in Jezreel. I can almost hear these people identifying themselves to Jehu as "relatives of Ahaziah." Did they think this would impress Jehu? It most certainly got a response from him! Jehu had Ahaziah's relatives seized and then put to death in the cistern at Beth Eked. He left no survivors. Judah's king and his relatives had chosen to make an alliance with Joram and his family, and now they would also participate in God's judgment upon the house of Ahab.

Jehu encountered someone else on the road to Samaria—Jehonadab, the son of Rekab, also referred to as Jonadab in the Bible. This man is not put to death; indeed, he is embraced by Jehu as a "kindred spirit." The character of this guy is alluded to in Jeremiah 35:

The LORD spoke to Jeremiah when Jehoiakim son of Josiah was ruling over Judah. He said, "Go to the

Rechabite community. Invite them to come into one of the side rooms of the temple of the LORD and offer them some wine to drink." So I went and got Jaazaniah, the son of Jeremiah, the grandson of Habazziniah, and his brothers and all his sons and all the rest of the Rechabite community. I took them to the temple of the LORD. I took them into the room where the disciples of the prophet Hanan son of Igdaliah stayed. That room was next to the one where the temple officers waited and above the room where Maaseiah son of Shallum, one of the doorkeepers of the temple, stayed. Then I set cups and pitchers full of wine in front of the members of the Rechabite community and said to them, "Have some wine," because our ancestor Jonadab, son of Rechab commanded us not to. He told us, "You and your children must never drink wine. Don't build houses. Don't plant crops. Don't plant a vineyard or own one. Live in tents all your lives. If you do these things you will live a long time in the land that you wander about on." We and our wives and our sons and daughters have obeyed everything our ancestor Jonadab commanded us. We have never drunk wine. We haven't built any houses to live in. We don't own any vineyards, fields, or crops. We have lived in tents. We have obeyed our ancestor Jonadab and done as he commanded us. But when

Nebuchadnezzar king of Babylon invaded the land we said, "Let's get up and go to Jerusalem to get away from the Babylonian and Aramean armies." That is why we are staying here in Jerusalem" (Jeremiah 35:1-11).

Jeremiah refers to "Jonadab son of Rechab" as an example of a man of character. His descendants were instructed by him not to drink wine, and even in Jeremiah's day, they refused to do so. Jeremiah will go on to argue that while the descendants of Jonadab insisted upon obeying the instructions of their forefather, the people of Judah and Jerusalem pay no regard at all to God's commandments. Jonadab is therefore represented in a favorable light; he is a man of principle and character, and so are his descendants.

When Jehu comes upon Jehonadab (Jonadab), he may have recognized him as someone he knew. His way of dealing with him is just the opposite of the way he dealt with the friends and family of Ahaziah. Jehu asks Jehonadab if he is a kindred spirit and Jehonadab assures him that he is. Jehu then takes him by the hand and takes him up into his chariot, so that he can accompany him and observe his zeal for carrying out God's instructions. Jehonadab will witness firsthand Jehu's dealings with the Baal worshipers of Samaria.

In Samaria, Jehu makes another bold move—one that will rid Israel of the Baal worship that Ahab and Jezebel had introduced. It was Omri, Ahab's father, who purchased the land and built the capital city of Samaria (1 Kings 16:23-24). And it was Ahab who built the house where Baal worship took place in the city (1 Kings 16:31-32). If Jehu's "house cleaning" was to be complete, he must rid Israel of the Baal worship Ahab had introduced.

Once again, we need to ponder the difficulty of the task at hand. If you were given the assignment of identifying all the Baal worshipers in the country and executing them, how would you do it? How would you identify them? How would you track them down and execute them? Jehu did not pursue the Baal worshipers; he got them to come to him. When Jehu arrived in Samaria, no one there was likely to have known about his God-given mission. His words may not have surprised anyone, and they would have delighted the Baal worshipers: If they thought Ahab was a Baal worshiper, they had not seen anything yet. Jehu promised to outdo the "king" of Baal worship.

It did not appear to be wise to offend Jehu. The heads had already begun to roll, literally, and no one wanted to be next. The Baal worshipers were probably ecstatic. Since the appearance of Elijah and Elisha, Baal worship may have begun to dwindle, but now there was a king who said that he would make Baal worship bigger and better than it had ever been. All of the prophets of Baal, their servants, and the pagan priests were gathered for the great celebration Jehu had prepared. No Baal worshiper was allowed to be absent. No Yahweh-worshiper has been authorized to be present.

Jehu did not have to search for the worshipers of Baal; they all came to him, eagerly. They made no attempt to conceal their identity as those who served Baal. Indeed, with a king like Jehu, they could worship openly and be proud of it, or so they thought. They arrived from all over Israel. Jehu ordered that each worshiper be given a robe to wear that designated them as one of the Baal worshipers. What the people who wore them didn't know was that this was a foolproof way of marking them for execution. It was almost like going into battle with only a T-shirt on one's chest, with a bull's eye painted on it, front and back.

Jehu made one last check to make certain that no servant of the LORD was among the Baal worshipers. He then offered the sacrifice and ordered his soldiers to go into the house of Baal and kill every Baal worshiper. Not one servant of the LORD perished that day, and not one Baal worshiper escaped. The soldiers then removed the sacred pillar of Baal and burned it. They destroyed the temple of Baal, and then, as a final desecration of this heathen temple, they turned it into a latrine. The Baal worship that Ahab and Jezebel had introduced to Israel was eradicated that very day.

"My Way" as Performed by King Jehu
(2 Kings 10:29-36)

I don't think Jehu had blue eyes like Frank Sinatra who popularized the "My Way" song; but in some things, Jehu carried out the message of the song, ignoring God's instructions and doing things his way. Jehu did not repudiate the sins that Jeroboam son of Nebat had encouraged Israel to commit; the golden calves remained in Bethel and Dan. However, God rewarded Jehu's obedience by allowing his sons to rule over Israel for the next four generations. To me, this shows God's mercy and faithfulness to honor Jehu for his obedience. The LORD said to Jehu, "You have done well. You have accomplished my will and carried out my wishes regarding Ahab's dynasty. Therefore, four generations of your descendants will rule over Israel."

But Jehu did not carefully and wholeheartedly obey the law of the LORD God of Israel. He did not repudiate the sins which Jeroboam had encouraged Israel to commit. In those days, the Lord began to reduce the size of Israel's territory. Hazael attacked their eastern border. He conquered all the land of Gilead, including the territory of Gad, Reuben, and Manasseh, extending all the way from the Aroer in the Arnon Valley through Gilead to Bashan. The rest of the events of Jehu's reign are recorded in the scroll called the *Annals of the Kings of Israel*. Jehu passed away and was buried in Samaria. His son Jehoahaz replaced him as king. Jehu reigned over Israel for 28 years in Samaria.

Jehu accomplished some remarkable tasks. Let's review what it was that he was commissioned to do:

This is what the LORD God of Israel says, "I have designated to reign as king over the LORD's people Israel. You will destroy the family of your master Ahab. I will get revenge against Jezebel for the shed blood of my servants the prophets and the shed blood of all the LORD's servants. Ahab's entire family will die. I will cut off every last male belonging to Ahab in Israel, including even the weak and incapacitated. I will make Ahab's dynasty like those of Jeroboam, son of Nebat and Baasha, son of Ahijah. Dogs will devour Jezebel in the plot of ground in Jezreel; she will not be buried" (2 Kings 9:6b-10).

It looks to me as though Jehu has completely fulfilled his mission, as the young prophet defined it. And from the final words of chapter 10, it seems that God agrees: The LORD said to Jehu, "You have done well. You have accomplished my will and carried out my wishes with regard to Ahab's dynasty. Therefore, four generations of your descendants will rule over Israel" (2 Kings 10:30).

God evaluated the first days of Jehu's reign as king of Israel. He was given a mission, and he carried it out entirely. The next words are not a direct statement from God, but are the author's inspired evaluation of the remainder of Jehu's life and reign as king of Israel—a reign of 28 years: "But Jehu did not carefully and wholeheartedly obey the law of the LORD God of Israel. Jehu did not repudiate the sins that Jeroboam had encouraged Israel to commit" (verse 31).

It is most interesting to read this evaluation of Jehu's life, compared to the assessment of some. They would have us believe that Jehu went too far, that he killed too many, and all for self-serving purposes. This assessment does not square with what God has said in verse 30. I'll settle for God's assessment. It's not surprising, though, that there are many that believe God would never deal severely with men, no matter how great their sin. But it is our sovereign God who sets the standards, and who rewards and punishes people by these criteria. It is not the severity of God's judgment which should distress us, but the immensity of man's sin. I am amazed at God's patience and longsuffering when I read the history of Israel. God repeatedly delayed his judgment and urged men to repent to avoid his wrath. In sending the prophets—they pointed out sin and its consequences—God called people to repent and avoid God's judgment.

How can this be, when we have just read that God commended Jehu for carrying out his directives regarding the house of Ahab? I think the answer comes in several parts. First, God's commendation was regarding a particular set of tasks, which were completed over a relatively short period. The author's condemnation is for Jehu's failures over the long haul, for the remainder of his 28-year reign.

The second part of the answer is bound up in a crucial principle: The believer's walk of faith and obedience is the walk of a lifetime. It is not measured merely regarding one's first acts of obedience, no matter how great those may be. Look at King Saul, for example. In the earliest days of his reign, Saul did well. He led Israel in the liberation of Jabesh-Gilead, defeating the Ammonites (1 Samuel 11). Shortly after that, things went downhill quickly. When evaluated by his first act of obedience, Saul did well; when assessed by his lifetime of leading Israel, Saul was a miserable failure.

I must issue a word of caution here. I do not mean to suggest that Jehu was a terrible king. He seems to be one of the best kings the northern kingdom of Israel ever had. He did well in ridding Israel of the false worship introduced by Ahab and Jezebel, but he failed badly in not doing away with the false religion established by Jeroboam.

There is a third factor here as well: Jehu did well in carrying out every command that was specifically addressed to him, but he did not do well in the discharge of the more general commands of God, namely the law. You may remember that God spoke about the need for kings to ponder and to obey the whole law:

"When you come to the land the LORD your God is giving you, and you take it over and live in it and then say, I will appoint a king over me like all the nations surrounding me, you must without fail select over you a king whom the LORD your God will choose. From among your kin, you must appoint a king—you may not designate a foreigner who is not one of your kin. Moreover, he must not accumulate horses for himself nor allow the people to return to Egypt to do so, for the LORD has said, you must never again return this way. He also must not marry many wives lest his affections turn aside, and he must not amass much silver and gold. When he sits on his royal throne, then he must make a copy of this instruction upon a scroll given to him by the Levitical priests. It must be constantly with him and he must read it as long as he lives so that he might learn to revere the LORD his God, and observe all the words of this instruction and these statutes in order to carry them out, so that he will not exalt himself above his fellow citizens and turn from the commandment right or left, and so that he might

enjoy many years over his kingdom, he and his descendants, in the midst of Israel (Deuteronomy 17:14-20)."

Contrasting King David and Jehu

What a difference there is between David and Jehu. Jehu obeyed only those commands addressed specifically to him. David sought to obey every command of God, not just the times when God spoke directly to him, but when God spoke in principle or precept through his Word. He sought to read between the lines and to discern the heart of God. He tried not only to avoid what would displease God and bring his discipline, but he endeavored to learn what pleased God and to do that.

There also may be another factor involved in Jehu's failure to deal with the false worship introduced by Jeroboam. Jeroboam's false religion had been around a lot longer than the Baal-ism submitted by Ahab and Jezebel. Jeroboam's false religion was not a "foreign import," as Baal-ism was. He introduced a counterfeit version of the only true religion, the worship of Yahweh. I believe it was relatively easy to rid the nation of Baal worship, but the worship that Jeroboam established was the "national religion" of the northern kingdom. When patriotism, nationalism, and religion are merged, it is not healthy. One may be reluctant to deal with a religious error because it is a part of one's culture and national identity.

The consequences for Jehu's failure were not as dramatic as God's judgment on the house of Ahab, but they were nonetheless painful and apparent. God began to nibble away at Israel's borders, reducing its size, power, and stature. Hazael attacked from the east, conquering the land of Gilead, and seizing property in the territory of God, Reuben, and Manasseh. Disobedience always has consequences. Jehu's life is summed up in but two chapters. His days of glory, though few, dominate the text devoted to him. His failure and its consequences are described in very few words.

Here Is the Bottom Line

Ahab and Jezebel had blood on their hands; therefore, their judgment was bloody. Israel's sacrificial system made this very apparent. Our Lord's death on the cross was a cruel and bloody death. He suffered in our place, to bear the penalty for our sins. If we acknowledge our sin and guilt and trust in the death and resurrection of Jesus Christ, we will not suffer God's eternal wrath, because Jesus has already done so. From a Jewish perspective, Jesus became our Passover Lamb. But if we reject his work on Calvary, our judgment will be severe, because America has a bloody, unrighteous past too. For example, how many "fetuses" have been aborted in America with our country's blessing! According to the latest statistics, the Bible says that life begins at the fertilization of the embryo, not at birth. An estimated 58,586,256 fetuses – the Bible calls them "babies" – have been aborted since 1973. The Bible calls that murder. Talk about bloody! Jehu's dealings with the sins of the house of Ahab should be a warning to us concerning how serious God is about judging sin and sinners.

If you have a problem with the word, "judgment," then consider the words "sowing and reaping" in Galatians 6:7-8 where it says:

Be not deceived; God is not mocked: for whatsoever a man soweth, that shall he also reap. For he that soweth to his flesh shall of the flesh reap corruption; but he that soweth to the Spirit shall of the Spirit reap life everlasting.

All people on earth are subject to the law of sowing and reaping.

I was thinking about modern warfare and the principle of sowing and reaping. During the war in the Persian Gulf, the United States used what we call "smart" missiles or bombs. We were shown photographs of direct hits on various targets. And yet there have also been some very tragic misses. A number have suffered and died because of a misguided bomb. As good as our military technology is, we still killed some innocent victims. However, Jehu managed to hit every target, without a miss. God's judgment is precise.

The Baal worshipers of Samaria are a tragic illustration of sinners who rush to their destruction. They couldn't get to Samaria fast enough to worship Baal. They eagerly put on their robes, which marked them for destruction. Sin blinds us to its consequences. We think that it offers us pleasure, but it leads us to destruction: *My child, do not go in the way with them, withhold your foot from their path; for their feet run to evil, and they hasten to shed blood; for it is futile to spread a net in front of all the birds! But these men lie in wait for their own blood, they lie in hiding for their own lives. Thus is the end of all who unjustly gain profit; it takes away the life of those who get it. Wisdom calls out in the street, she lifts up her voice in the plazas; at the head of the noisy streets she calls, in the entrances of the gates in the city she makes her speech: "How long will you simpletons love simple ways? How long will mockers delight in mockery, and fools hate knowledge? If only you will respond to my rebuke, then I will pour out my spirit to you, and I will make my thoughts known to you. Since I called but you refused me, I stretched out my hand but no one paid attention, and you neglected all my advice and did not comply with my rebuke, then I will laugh at your disaster, I will mock when what you dread comes, when what you dread comes like a whirlwind, and your disaster comes like a storm, when distress and trouble come upon you. Then they will call to me, but I will not answer; they will look to me, but they will not find me. Because they hated knowledge and did not choose the fear of the LORD, they did not comply with my advice, they spurned all my rebukes, then they will eat from the fruit of their way and from their counsel they will be satisfied. For the turning away of the simple will kill them, and the careless ease of fools will destroy them. But the one who listens to me will live in security and be at ease from the dread of harm"* (Proverbs 1:15-33).

My child pay attention to my wisdom, incline your ear to my understanding in order to safeguard discretion, and that your lips may guard knowledge. For the lips of the adulteress woman drip honey, and her mouth is smoother than oil, but in the end she is bitter like wormwood, sharp as a two-edged sword. Her feet go down to death; her steps lead straight to the grave. Lest she should make level the path of life her paths are unstable, but she does not know it. So now, children, listen to me; do not turn aside from the words of my mouth. Keep your way far from her, and do not go near the door of her house" (Proverbs 5:1-8).

Like the wisdom in these proverbs, the prophets continually proclaimed the truth, exposed sin, and warned of coming judgment. And like the foolish ones, the Baal worshipers of Israel plunged headlong to their destruction. I believe the same thing is about to happen in America.

> **Sin always _takes you_ farther than you want to go, _keeps you_ longer than you want to stay, and _costs you_ more than you want to pay. Obedience to God is wisdom that leads to blessings, success, and prosperity (Author Unknown).**

> **Wisdom Key:**
> Sin always _takes you_ farther than you want to go, _keeps you_ longer than you want to stay, and _costs you_ more than you want to pay. Obedience to God is wisdom that leads to blessings, success, and prosperity (Author Unknown).

Chapter 7: What's Next for America?

> *Israel became a nation because I loved them. But, America became a nation because they loved me! Like Israel, I have a covenant with the American Founders. I haven't forgotten that!*
>
> *I have heard the prayers of my people, and I'm healing the land of America. America is not just about to have another Great Awakening. America is about to have a Reformation.*

The New Wine Is Coming!

I believe that the old wine skin (the traditional way of doing things) has been focused toward building a well-located building and believing "they will come." I call that the Church Retail Store. They have a more "Y'all Come" mantra. Many churches have even created TV commercials to attract members. That wine skin was limited to a gift-driven focus and a Spirit-led paradigm at best. A problem with that church model is that it draws "members" who follow the teachings of a well know minister. But God wants the church to attract disciples who will follow after *relationships*. That's because the former wine skin's limitations tend toward performance and works, rather than relational-dependence on the Holy Spirit.

For example, what if you get an accurate word from God, but you don't have the right timing? You might think, God wouldn't have given it to me if he didn't want me to give it to them! Further, the gift-centered focus tends to disqualify those that aren't gifted in the way leaders think they should be. So, the leaders exercise their authority and quench the spirit of that movement of God. That's because that old wine skin can't host the new wine. I saw that happen several times as I served as a part-time Youth and Music Director while attending college.

At a church during my first official part-time Youth and Music Director position, we enjoyed the simplicity of worshiping God, sharing testimonies and listening to the Spirit of God speak to us corporately. Afterward, we would respond appropriately. And our worship was primarily in homes. We were focused on what the Spirit of God was saying to our small group, rather than on what someone else was saying or trying to teach us. Today, I call that the "Presence Driven Life" new end-time wine skin. Rick Warren wrote an excellent book about *The Purpose Driven Life*. I believe God is changing The Purpose Driven Life mantra that was gift-driven to The Presence Driven Life that will be presence driven. Therefore, our new wine skin of the end-time focus is about learning how to host and release the manifest *presence of God* as Jesus and the 12 Apostles did.

Do you remember the Ark of the Covenant? Anywhere the Ark went, the "host" was dramatically blessed. That's a picture of the end-time wine skin, The Presence Driven Life. The former old wine skin was purpose- and gift-driven and that life tended toward personal performance. But the New Wine, The Presence Driven Life, will be about the presence of God, releasing the Kingdom of God everywhere we take it, with words of prophecy that will change lives, environments and circumstances.

Jesus said, *"Verily, verily, I say unto you, He that believeth on me, the works that I do shall he also do; and greater works than these shall he do; because I go unto my Father. And whatsoever ye shall ask in my name, that will I do, that the Father may be glorified in the Son" (John 14:12-13) (KJV).*

When Jesus said, "greater things you will do," I believe He was telling the apostles that they would do even greater things after He went to heaven, because He would send the Spirit of God to them. Many interpret those words as meaning that the apostles will do greater things than Jesus. But that's not what it's saying. It's saying that they (the apostles) will do more awesome things.

The new wine skin doesn't need a traditional religious building because it's birthed in the marketplace – in businesses – in schools – in restaurants – coffee houses, etc. This wine skin is the same as the original first-century wine skin during the time of Jesus and his 12 Apostles. In the New Testament, "the Church" becomes the "people". That means that everywhere the people of God go, the church goes. God's presence is no longer limited to a building or a Jewish Temple or the Arc of the Covenant. The spirit of God is now in the hearts of all believers as experienced on the Day of Pentecost. This fulfills the prophecy of Jeremiah 31:33 that says,

"*But this shall be the covenant that I will make with the house of Israel. After those days, saith the LORD, I will put my law in their inward parts, and write it in their hearts; and will be their God, and they shall be my people.*" (KJV)

Our new wine mantra is "The Presence Driven Life!"

"I only DO what I SEE my Father Do, and SAY what I hear him Say." (Jesus)

As we have learned, Elijah and Elisha were two of the most famous prophets of Israel. They both served in the northern kingdom of Israel. Elijah was first introduced in 1 Kings 17 as the prophet who predicted a three-year drought in the land. After being miraculously fed by ravens, he later stayed with a widow and her son, and that family experienced God's supernatural provision of food.

After Elijah defeated the prophets of Baal by calling down fire from heaven, the drought ended. Rain fell, and Elijah fled from the evil Queen Jezebel, who had vowed to kill him (1 Kings 19). Reaching Mount Horeb, Elijah heard the voice of God tell him to anoint two kings as well as Elisha as a prophet. He did this, and Elisha immediately joined him (1 Kings 19:19-21).

Elijah later condemned King Ahab for murder and the theft of a vineyard and predicted Ahab's death and that of his wife, Jezebel (1 Kings 21:17-24).

In 2 Kings 1, Elijah called down fire from heaven to destroy two groups of 50 men sent from King

Ahaziah. A third group of men was led by a captain who begged for mercy and was spared judgment. Elijah went to Ahaziah and proclaimed that the king would die from his sickness, a prophecy that was soon fulfilled.

In 2 Kings 2, Elijah and Elisha crossed the Jordan River on dry land, and Elisha, knowing that Elijah would not be with him much longer, asked to be blessed with a double portion of Elijah's spirit. Elijah was taken directly into heaven by a chariot of fire. Elisha picked up Elijah's mantle and used it to cross the Jordan again on dry land. He received the double portion he had asked for and performed many miracles in Israel. One of Elisha's miracles was the turning of bad water into clean water (2 Kings 2:19–22). A second, causing a widow's oil to fill many jars (2 Kings 4:1–7). A third, raising a boy from the dead (2 Kings 4:32–37).

Before he was taken to heaven in a chariot, Elijah left a letter for King Jehoram of Judah that spoke of judgment against him. It stated, in part, "The LORD will bring a great plague on your people, your children, your wives, and all your possessions, and you will have a severe sickness with a disease of your bowels, until your bowels come out because of the disease, day by day" (2 Chronicles 21:14–15). The prophecy soon came true (verses 18–20). Elijah and Elisha were greatly respected by those in the "school of prophets" (2 Kings 2 and 4:38–41) as well as by the kings of their nation. Their impact led to a revival among some of the Israelites during a dark stage of its history. During the evil reigns of Ahab and Ahaziah, God had his men leading the charge for righteousness.

God also has people that are leading the charge for purity in America today. But like Jehu during the time of Elijah and Elisha, they are the unlikely leaders of the "marketplace," not the well-known religious leaders of the past. The age of the "big name" of men, religion, and human-made things is over.

We will see an increase of home churches and marketplace-based ministries focused on the big name of Jesus and the end-time, during which people will see the supernatural power of God through his children. It's time for the restoration of all things, including the rebirthing of the Jewish roots of Christianity that will usher in an increase of miracles, signs, and wonders. Just as at the end of Queen Jezebel's reign, Israel was reborn, so it will be in America, a reformation and a great awakening after which America will never be the same. Historically, the only reformation that has caught most Americans' attention was the Great Reformation of the 1500's with Martin Luther. That served to birth the Protestant Church movement and eventually became an incentive for believers to travel to America in 1776.

For many years, the Catholic Church was empowered by a partnership with the Roman Empire called "The Holy Roman Empire". It was a time when the Roman Catholic Church exercised considerable influence over the Roman Emperor and Rome. The process of creating their version of Christianity started in about 325 AD after the Roman Emperor, Constantine, made Christianity the state religion of Rome. Emperor Constantine's actions of creating Christianity in his own image eventually birthed a "universal" Christian church in Rome; thus, the name Roman Catholic later began to take its place in history. In other words, the name Catholic Church means "Universal Church." But today, we can see that, by definition, Catholicism is simply another Christian denomination or sect, because the first 300 years of Christianity featured a distinctly Jewish worship liturgy and fellowship.

During the first 300 years of Christianity, even the "Gentiles" that believed in Jesus Christ honored the "Jewish Feasts" and the Sabbath as individual appointments with God, not just dead religious activities that passed away with the law.

According to Jewish history written by Jews, God intended that special blessings that he promised to obedient Jews would be transferred to the obedient Gentiles through their faith in Christ. That's what Galatians 3:29 says: *"And if ye be Christ's, then are ye Abraham's seed, and heirs according to the promise. Now to Abraham and his seed were the promises made. He saith not, And to seeds, as of many; but as of one, And to thy seed, which is Christ."* Galatians 3:16 (KJV).

> **Wisdom Key:**
> **What we honor will increase. What we dishonor will decrease.**

As I have previously stated, the first 300 years of Christianity were distinctly Jewish. Starting in AD 325 with Roman Emperor Constantine and lasting about 1200 years, the universal Christian church was dominated by the State-supported Roman Catholic Church. However, there was still a remnant of believers who practiced their Christian faith outside of the Roman Catholic Church, while honoring and preserving the original Jewish version of Christianity. After all, the Christian Messiah was a Jew for a reason.

It's up to the spiritually hungry to find out those reasons and the significances of Jesus being a Jew. And then, we need to embrace everything God wants us to know about Jewish roots to enable us to be all God wants us to be and do all God wants us to do. That's learning how to have a Kingdom of God mindset based on God's unconditional love and humility, rather than a narcissistic know-it-all, religious focus founded in pride and tradition.

When the church in Rome began to emphasize working for their salvation and giving monetary gifts for "spiritual favors," many followers of Christ, like Martin Luther, were troubled by their greed, hypocrisy and corruption. As a result, Martin Luther led a reformation that made way for the modern Protestant churches to explode in growth, permanently changing religion and politics and inadvertently making way for the formation of the Holy Roman Empire. Some of my ancestors were

Protestants who migrated from France to the land of opportunity – the USA.

The Death of the Early Church

Have you ever wondered why Christians and local churches today are very different from the time of Jesus and the 12 Apostles? And have you wondered why American Christians honor all of the Ten Commandments but one? And perhaps you have wondered why Jesus and the Apostles accepted "the Jewish Feasts" and the Sabbath, but today's American churches don't? But most of all, have you ever wondered why we don't see the miracles, signs, and wonders today like they had during the early days of Christianity?

Have you ever stopped to consider that God and his word aren't the problems? Some theologians have made excuses for the modern churches' lack of power and miracles, as well as their general ignorance of the Bible. They claim that miracles aren't for today because only Jesus and the 12 Apostles could perform miracles, signs, and wonders. But like I told a good friend of mine that believes in Cessation Theology: "The primary difference between your Cessation Theology and what I believe is that you believe in limiting God; and I don't. And since Jesus said in Matthew 9:29, 'According to your faith be it unto you,' we're both right. If you believe miracles have passed away, according to your faith be it unto you. If you believe that miracles are for today, according to your faith be it unto you." Like a quote I heard many years ago, "If you believe you can or if you believe you can't, you're right." (Author Unknown)

I've learned not to limit God regardless of my lack of power or lack of anything. The revelation that I've received from studying the words of Jesus has changed everything. I've learned to exchange my doubts, fears and unbelief for the words found in the Bible, especially those spoken by Jesus, because Jesus had perfect theology.

Many years ago, I had a man challenge me to study only the words spoken by Jesus for a month. After that study, I was never the same again. I challenge you to focus on just the words spoken by Jesus.

In this chapter, I will offer some answers to these and other concerns. I think that you will find, as I have, that the Early Church was enjoying the power and miracles of God for about the first three hundred years, ending only when a particular event occurred.

I'll explain what I've learned about that in this chapter, entitled, as you might imagine, "The Death of the Early Church."

Christianity is more accurately called, Judeo-Christianity; because for about the first three hundred years of Christianity, the early followers of Jesus were distinctly Jewish and followers of Jesus the Messiah, who was also a Jew. According to the New Testament, Jesus and the Apostles honored the Sabbath and the Feasts, while training the Gentiles and the Jews to do the same.

When Paul was sent to Rome, a city of Gentiles, he continued to teach and make disciples, teaching them to believe that Jesus was the promised Messiah and was resurrected from the dead. Paul also taught them to honor the Sabbath and the Feasts, because he knew that they were Yahweh's (God's) feasts that were meant for all believers in Christ, not just "Jewish Feasts" as many Gentile believers teach today. But everything began to change under the Roman Emperor, Constantine.

First Known Separation of Church and State

Toward the end of the Roman Emperor Constantine's reign, he announced that Christianity was the official state religion but then began to create Christianity in his own image. Starting with the Council Nicea in 325 AD, Constantine rid the Roman Christian State Church of its Jewish influences and practices. And while Constantine was re-making Christianity to suit his own desires, he was also marrying paganism with his version of Christianity – probably to politically appease the pagans.

Like King Saul, Constantine did God's will *his* way, rather than strictly obeying what God said to do through the Jewish Prophets and *The Torah* (translated as "the teachings of God" in Hebrew, but "The Law" in most English versions). Constantine cut off the roots of Christianity along with the intended blessings that God wanted to give us. Another word for this is *compromise*, which is simply an excuse for disobedience. As a result, the first Christian Feasts that were honored by Jesus and the apostles were renamed the "Jewish Feasts." And once they became Jewish Feasts, it was no longer lawful for the only recognized Church of Rome to practice or partake of them. Does that sound familiar?

Because of the limited evidence of what the Church was like during the first years of its existence, people sometimes assume that Christianity was always like it is today. But, that is easily disproven. History confirms that there was a strong "Jewish Influence" in the early church, and that it existed until Constantine eliminated it from Christianity. There is also Biblical evidence that Jesus honored the "Feasts of Yahweh" and the Sabbath. When I couple what both history and God's Word presents regarding the early church, it is clear to me that the first three hundred years of Christianity included a much more convincing Jewish experience than Christianity exhibits today.

Following Constantine, there were many other Roman Emperors that continued Constantine's anti-Semitic decrees by systematically removing the Jewish influences that were a part of Christianity until all traces of the early church Jewish experiences were completely eliminated.

Interestingly, this was the time when the miracles, signs, and wonders began to fade, although, like today, there was a remnant of the faithful who continued to enjoy the power, miracles, signs and wonders promised by Jesus.

Constantine also began to separate the Feasts and the Sabbath as part of Judaism, apart from Christianity. Through the years, there were numerous other "Rome Councils," but it was Constantine who initiated the anti-Semitic decrees, which eventually led to abandoning "Jewish practices" in Christianity.

The Return to Jewish Roots

In the early years of Christianity, Christian followers honored the Jewish Feasts and the Sabbath. They also practiced a home-based discipleship and worship model that was designed to prepare the next generation to know Christ and to make him known. Their weekly home-based-family-based fellowship "church" model also included eating, praying, sharing, and studying the Torah (the first five books of the Bible). As a result, there were many miracles, signs and wonders by Jesus, the 12 Apostles and their disciples.

During this time, many people were being added to the church daily. While the Old Testament spoke of a temple built by man's hands, the New Testament model teaches that the people of God are the temple of God, because Jesus sent his Spirit to indwell and empower all of those that chose to believe, receive and follow him.

Jesus did not attempt to establish a new religion. However, he did create a new way of life that included a supernatural component with miracles, signs, and wonders being performed through all who believed. Jesus also said, "According to your faith be it unto you." When they honored the words of Jesus, they enjoyed supernatural provision, signs, and wonders. But when they didn't accept the words of Jesus, only a few were healed because of their unbelief (Matthew 13:58).

The worship of the early church centered on home church fellowships, which focused on families, not institutionalized religious activities and duties. And so it was with the Feasts, the Sabbath, and all other teachings found in the Hebrew translation of the Torah, which is sometimes inadequately called "The Law" by many Christians today.

One of the most common misunderstandings of the Torah is found with those that have referred to it as "The Law", saying that "we're not under the law anymore, so we don't need to follow it." I believe that serves to dishonor the teachings of the Torah, which are more accurately translated as "the teachings of Yahweh (God, The Father)".

Jesus, the twelve Apostles and others that they trained, honored the Torah, The Feasts, and the Sabbath. Therefore, they enjoyed the "benefits" of accepting God's teachings as listed in Deuteronomy 28. But because of what Jesus did on the cross, they didn't have to live under the *curse* of the law. Jesus did away with the curses of the law, but not the blessings of the law.

What were the benefits and blessings of the law? According to the New Testament, all of the 12 Apostles and the 120 trainees worked miracles of healing along with signs and wonders, while enjoying supernatural provision.

If you would like to study more about Christianity's Jewish Roots, I highly recommend Dr. Robert D. Heidler's book, *The Messianic Church Arising!* ISBN: 0-9791678-2-5.

According to the original and literal Hebrew translation in Leviticus 23, "the Jewish Feasts" were not Jewish, and they were not just feasts. They were

"God's Appointed Times" for the Jews and later the Christians to meet annually with God.

Here is what God said to Moses about the Feasts in Leviticus 23 (NKJV).

The Feasts of the Lord

"And the Lord spoke to Moses, saying, 'Speak to the children of Israel, and say to them: 'The feasts of the Lord, which you shall proclaim *to be* holy convocations, **these *are* My feasts**.'"

The Sabbath

"Six days shall work be done, but the **seventh day *is* a Sabbath of solemn rest, a holy convocation**. You shall do no work *on it;* it *is* the Sabbath of the Lord in all your dwellings."

The Passover and Unleavened Bread

"These *are* the feasts of the Lord, holy convocations which you shall proclaim at their appointed times.

- The Feast of First Fruits
- The Feast of Weeks
- The Feast of Trumpets
- The Day of Atonement
- The Feast of Tabernacles

"So Moses declared to the children of Israel <u>the feasts of the Lord</u>."(NKJV)

How do we restore the power of God to the Body of Christ? And how do we "stop the bleeding" of our young American people exiting our churches and abandoning their faith in Christ? The Presidential election may reflect how many Americans voted to restore Biblical principles, rather than considering what "freebies" they could get from our government.

> **Wisdom Key:**
> **"When the people discover they can vote themselves money from the US Treasury, it will be the end of the Republic." John Quincy Adams**

The Rebirthing and Reformation of America

A great awakening is beginning. It will open America's eyes to the goodness of God and the foolishness and corruption of Americans, especially through government. Like Romans 2:4 says, *"the goodness of God leads to repentance."* And Jeremiah 17:9 says, *"The heart is deceitful above all things, and desperately wicked: who can know it?"*

America is about to experience a significant pruning, like in John 15, that will lead to the American

Reformation and the re-birthing of America! Here's how it will start.

In my quiet time with God, I heard the following:

Son, I'm doing a new thing. The old wine skin cannot host the new wine that I'm pouring out during these days. So, I'm changing the old wine skin that was gift-driven and enabled a performance paradigm to a Presence Driven lifestyle that will enable a "whatever-God-Says-I'll-Do/Say" focus. My people will gather to worship me and listen to what my spirit is saying to them, rather than only listening to what a speaker/pastor/teacher is saying to them.

Moses never saw the Promised Land. But Joshua led God's people into the land of milk and honey. God told me that WE are the new Joshua Generation and that it was time to take back the Promised Land! This means the end of the big-name denominations, bestselling authors, celebrities and any other man-made thing, including the current religious institutional focus. People's homes and the marketplace are where I'm moving. The Purpose Driven Life focus is changing to a Presence Driven Life focus!

No longer will men take undue credit for what I am doing on the earth. That's why I am pruning the hearts of my people, enabling them to humble themselves, pray, seek my face and turn from their own ways to activate my word, will, and ways.

These days will be about the "big name" of Jesus and the rebirthing of the "big name" of the Body of Christ that assembles together to honor God's Biblical protocols in his word, will, and ways. A book that began to open my eyes to some of these new end-time truths was *The Day of the Saints*, by Dr. Bill Hamon. I also learned from Dr. Heidler's book, *The Messianic Church Arising*, and enjoyed his enlightenment that God is restoring the Jewish roots to the body of Christ.

The first protocol we need to honor is 2 Chronicles 7:14: If my people will (1) humble themselves, (2) pray, (3) seek my face and (4) turn from their wicked ways, I will (A) hear their prayers, (B) forgive their sins and (C) heal their land.

Many have said that God will have to destroy America or apologize to Sodom and Gomorra because of our corruption. But the condition of America is much different from Sodom and Gomorrah! How? God told Abraham that he would spare Sodom and Gomorrah if he could find ten righteous men. But he couldn't! And Sodom and

Gomorrah was destroyed. However, it is different for America. I submit to you that there are thousands, perhaps even hundreds of thousands or maybe even millions of righteous people in America right now. If you don't see that, perhaps this is an Elijah on the Mountain of Carmel moment for you?

Although Elijah was greatly discouraged by his circumstances, God said to Elijah in 1 Kings 18-19, *"You're not the only one left. There are still many that have not bowed their knees to Baal."* I believe that is also true about America today. Following the US Supreme Court decision on Gay marriage, many American leaders are having an Elijah on Mt. Carmel experience. And, I believe that God is saying the same thing to us that he said to Elijah. Can you hear him?

During my evening Bible meditation, the Holy Spirit began to share with me about what he is doing in America - very soon. He said that he has heard the prayers of his people and will allow America to survive the impending Perfect Storm, although many will doubt and wonder if America will survive. Some will even expect God's judgment and destruction on America because of her wickedness. But, I believe that the Lord is about to prune America like he prunes a vine as described in John 15, not destroy her, although there will be severe consequences for America's wickedness.

America will never be the same again. She will lose her worldwide dominion and world reserve currency status. And like Great Britain (the Lion) before her, I believe America (the wings of an eagle) will be allowed to remain for a season as mentioned in Daniel 7. I will share more about America in Bible prophecy later in this chapter.

What will the pruning of America look like? In John 15, God clarified the purpose of the pruning process. When a branch doesn't bear fruit, he prunes it to enable it to bear fruit. Or when a branch bears a little fruit, he prunes it to bear more fruit. And when a branch bears more fruit, he prunes it to bear much fruit. Has this ever happened to you? It certainly has to me! I believe that God has pruned America in the past too.

When trees are being pruned, if they could talk, they might say things like, "Not that one God! That was my favorite! What good can come out of pruning that one?" They might say, "God! There's nothing left!" or "What am I going to do now?" or "No one will even notice me now." Or they might lament the damage, crying, "They will certainly reject me without that."

In the words of a big hit song written by Chris Kristopherson, trees enduring pruning might ask, "Why Me Lord? What have I ever done?"

Bible Characters that God Pruned

Joseph, betrayed by his brothers, was being pruned to eventually become the second in command of all Egypt. But before that could happen, Joseph had to endure being sold by his brothers to slave traders, purchased by Potiphar and treated like a slave in Potiphar's house, falsely accused by Potiphar's wife, and caused to live many years in prison because of false allegations against him. Eventually Joseph interpreted Pharaoh's dream, which finally opened the door for Joseph to become the second in command over Egypt. All of this, I believe, was the result of God's pruning in Joseph's life.

Because Joseph responded to God's pruning according to 2 Chronicles 7:14, God was able to bless him beyond his wildest imagination. How? Joseph humbled himself by becoming teachable; he prayed to God, he sought the face of God and turned from his own ways of thinking and doing, while embracing God's Word, Will and Ways. And none of this could have happened without God's pruning, because each misfortune in Joseph's life took him one step closer to second in command over all of Egypt!

If we don't humble ourselves (to become flexible and teachable) like Joseph during pruning, the Vinedresser will have to cut us off permanently (Proverbs 29: 1). And, perhaps Jesus cursed the fig tree for the same reason? (See Mark 11: 13)

In my walk with God, he has removed (cut off) specific jobs, circumstances and people in my life that I thought were helpful and sometimes even needed; after which, I even experienced a time of loss and grief in some cases. I've learned that this is part of following Jesus as he asked us to do in Matthew 16:24, "Then said Jesus unto his disciples, 'If any man will come after me, let him deny himself, and take up his cross, and follow me.'"

Does God Prune Nations Too?

The War between Great Britain and the early settlers of America was a pruning war. Great Britain was greatly humbled by their bitter defeat. After all, Great Britain had dominion over all the earth up until that time. They had the most powerful navy in the world. Perhaps Great Britain's prominence as a nation for so many years is primarily why the English Language is the default language of the world today.

Many countries taught English as a second language because knowing the language of Great Britain was required to trade commerce and to do business. Plus, the missionaries taught them English. In addition, the English "Pound" was the world's reserve currency, meaning that all countries and people had to exchange their countries' currencies into the pound before they could trade and do business in the world.

However, after World Wars 1 and 2, the American US Dollar replaced the English Pound as the world's reserve currency. So, the result of God's pruning of Great Britain was to humble them and cause them to lose their world dominion, I believe, because of their wickedness. On the other hand, the pruning of America in both World Wars caused the USA to bear much fruit and to enjoy a time of unprecedented prosperity and promotion, the American dollar replacing the British Pound as the world's reserve currency.

Of course, most of us are more familiar with God pruning the individual Christian. Perhaps you've never considered the possibility of God pruning a nation. But think about it. God pruned the Hebrews and Israelites, while they were in the desert. And the Great Commission exhorts Christians "to make disciples of all nations" (Matthew 28: 16-20). And as John 15 teaches, pruning is a necessary "evil" for us to bear fruit, more fruit and much fruit.

In Matthew 28, God prunes people and nations as a normal part of the discipleship process. He prunes any time that there is a group of people that has (at one time) believed and honored his Word, Will and Ways, i.e. his covenant. For example, in Genesis, God pruned (removed) the entire population of the earth, except Noah and his family. This enabled the earth to get a fresh start and to begin accomplishing God's original purpose for mankind which was to be fruitful, multiply and take dominion over all the earth.

Over the rich history of Israel, we can see how God pruned them to bear fruit/more fruit/much fruit. Simply put, God prunes those branches that bear fruit so they can produce more fruit. And he prunes them again so that they can bear much fruit. But the branches that do not bear any fruit, God removes them - permanently.

Is America Mentioned in Bible Prophecy?

Are there any Bible verses that support America's participation during end-time events? Absolutely! I am convinced that the USA is mentioned in the Old and New Testaments after listening to Irvin Baxter teach this. And, it appears that America has a specific part to play during the Great Tribulation! Here's my evidence: There are two chapters in the Bible in which USA and Israel are mentioned as a part of prophecy: Daniel 7 and Revelation 12. In Daniel 7, Daniel's dream provided a perfect allegory of the rise and fall of America, along with the consequences that America and other modern nations would experience for their wickedness.

Here's what Daniel 7:4 says:

The first was like a lion, and it had the wings of an eagle. I watched until its wings were torn off and it was lifted from the ground so that it stood on two feet like a human being, and the mind of a human was given to it.

The phrase "wings of a great eagle", I believe, is referring to America who uses the eagle as her national bird. The eagle is on our flag and our currency. Then the scripture goes on to say, "I watched until its wings were torn off". This is a perfect description of how America was formed – torn from her mother country, the Lion, Great Britain. The word "torn" implies pain, spilled blood and military battles.

The next words in Daniel 7 are, "*and it was lifted from the ground so that it stood on two feet like a human being, and the mind of a human was given to it.*" Again, this is a stunning and accurate description of Uncle Sam - the popular persona of the American Government. There is no other time in world history that this kind of understanding could have been realized.

Is there evidence that America will still be protecting Israel during the Great Tribulation? In Revelation 12:13, the dragon, Satan, is depicted making war against the woman, Israel. Then, Israel is rescued by the **two wings of a great eagle**.

And to the woman were given two wings of a great eagle that she might fly into the wilderness, into her place, where she is nourished for a time, and times, and half a time, from the face of the serpent. (Revelation 12:14)

America and Great Britain have been instrumental in enabling Israel to become a nation again. That officially happened in 1947. And America has been militarily protecting Israel, while acting as a safe haven for Jews to prosper since her founding in 1776. Revelation 12:14 seems to indicate that America will be a power to reckon with even during the Great Tribulation, although America won't have world dominion - just as Daniel 7 says. The words **a time, and times, and half a time** in Revelation 12:14 are believed to be referring to the 3 ½ years of the Great Tribulation.

In my opinion, America has at least two assignments from God: (1) Take the Gospel to all the world, while discipling the nations and (2) Bless Israel. There has been no other nation in the history of the world that has simultaneously fulfilled both of those assignments like America. And like a diamond in the rough, America will be cut by the Master's hand until the sparkle of the Glory of God can once again be seen by the whole world. The true Body of Christ will become a beacon of light and the salt of the earth. This will serve to make the way for the last, Joel 2, spiritual revolution on the earth right before the second coming of Jesus Christ.

John 15 (NKJV) - The True Vine

I am the true vine, and My Father is the vinedresser. 2 Every branch in Me that does not bear fruit He takes away; and every branch that bears fruit He prunes, that it may bear more fruit. 3 You are already clean because of the word which I have spoken to you. 4 Abide in Me, and I in you. As the branch cannot bear fruit of itself, unless it abides in the vine, neither can you, unless you abide in Me. 5 "I am the vine, you are the branches. He who abides in Me, and I in him, bears much fruit; for without Me you can do nothing. 6 If anyone does not abide in Me, he is cast out as a branch and is withered; and they gather them and throw them into the fire, and they are burned. 7 If you abide in Me, and My words abide in you, you will ask what you desire, and it shall be done for you. 8 By this My Father is glorified, that you bear much fruit; so, you will be My disciples.

How Is God Pruning America?

- In short, America is not just having a Great Awakening. America is having a Reformation!

- The next move of God will cause America to be Reborn!

- God is pruning hearts and looking for fathers with clean hands and a pure heart, not just teachers. All good fathers can teach, but not all good teachers can father. A father reproduces himself and makes a name for his sons. But, a teacher doesn't reproduce and makes a name for himself.

- God is pruning the hearts of all that will respond and submit to him.

- It's time to make disciples, not church members. A church member looks for teachings, but a disciple looks for relationships. That's why Jesus said, "Follow Me," rather than encouraging people to just intellectually agree with a doctrine.

First, like John 15 teaches, the branches that do not bear fruit will be cut off and lose their influence in America. That will happen in all areas of American culture, because God has heard our prayers, forgiven our sin and is healing our land (2 Chronicles 7: 14).

Just as God raised up a leader and the "sons of the prophets" during the Prophet Elisha's time, so is God raising up a leader and a company of prophetic people to prophesy (with Kingly intercessory prayer) to the spirits of Jezebel and Ahab that they are to be cut off (pruned) and to be permanently removed from all governmental authority in America. This Kingly-prophetic authority will also decree the leader that God is raising up that has the Jehu Factor operating in his life to take care of God's business – God's way.

And as it happened in ancient Israel, Americans will rebuild America to honor the Judeo-Christian principles that once shaped the foundation of American success and culture. Those ancient life principles that served as a foundation to American government were handed down from God, through the Jews and to America with Jesus as the Chief Cornerstone.

The Jehu Factor and Donald Trump

During pre-service prayer at my local church, a prayer partner of mine and I decided to pray for the fall 2015 fall primary elections in America. This was in August of 2015. As we were praying, I felt led to pray for Donald Trump's protection, although he was not my choice for President – Mike Huckabee was. And I heard the words, "Pray a hedge of protection around Donald Trump." So, remembering the days when I watched science fiction movies, we prayed a force field of protection around Donald Trump. We continued to pray that anything sent to harm him would bounce off of him and return to the one that sent it.

Shortly after that prayer in August of 2015, we began to notice people trying to slander Donald Trump through the usual mean-spirited commercials or slander, thinking they could harm him. However, the more negative they came out against him – the more his poll numbers increased. It was unbelievable to watch the hand of God answer our prayers to protect Donald Trump. Although he was not my choice for President, I thought, I don't want anything bad to happen to him or anyone else.

At another time, while praying for the healing of our nation, God began to speak to me, saying he had "heard our prayers of intercession for the healing of America and he was starting that process by pruning our land." He then reminded me of Jehu in 2 Kings, showing me that Donald Trump has been chosen by God to help remove the corruption in American politics in both major political parties.

Like Jehu, all that will respond to God's invitation to humble themselves, pray, seek his face and turn from their ways, will be in a position to be protected and to prosper during the coming pruning. Those that won't respond to God's invitation found in 2 Chronicles 7:14 will be cut off without remedy, and some will be put underneath the feet of men (John 15). Others will be pruned to bear fruit, more fruit, and much fruit, according to God's great wisdom.

As a result of this revelation, I wrote an article that appeared on my September 1, 2015, column called,

"The **Trump** Has Sounded"

Journalists all over the USA and all areas of the American media have been attempting to solve the mystery of Donald Trump's popularity and success as he continues to defy the political establishment and their politically correct machine. Some have called him a genius, while others have called him *a phenomenon* and still others have called him *rude, crude and dangerous*. The current political establishment has practiced their version of how to win elections and influence people. But Donald Trump has defied them while proving them to be wrong – again and again.

The Republican's politically correct police have lost the last two presidential elections to a senator that had never held a regular full-time job or even managed a small department in a retail store! And they want us to trust them to select the next RNC

Presidential candidate without them making any changes? And the DNC helped elect a US President that had one of the most radical and liberal voting records in the Congress when he served a short term as a Senator. Further, neither the DNC nor the FBT properly checked into his background. I had background checks that scrutinized me more when I applied to teach children! Further, I have not seen any evidence that the DNC or the federal government examined Barack Obama's background at all. It's time for both political party establishments to hand off the baton to the next generation! And I believe that Donald Trump is making way for that transfer of power to begin!

The Republican's you-scratch-my-back-and-I'll-scratch-yours approach has not been working for the American people; and the Democrats' Robin Hood "take-from-the-rich-and-give-to-the-poor" approach is only making things worse! The Republicans' approach has enabled "crony capitalism" and the Democrats' plan is destroying the middle class – as the rich keep getting richer and the poor keep getting more entitlements, while the middle class pays the price.

America Will Never Be the Same!

The two principal political parties in America, the Republicans and the Democrats, have done a great disservice to America! They have been more interested in promoting their self-interests and increasing their personal wealth and party power than in running the American government's business for the benefit of the American people! I believe the majority of Americans are aware of this and that knowledge serves as a lighthouse to help them navigate their way through the stormy seas of politics, continuing to light the path toward Donald Trump's political success.

To understand the dynamics of Mr. Trump's popularity, we can review the Biblical story of Elijah, Elisha and Jehu. The rulers over Israel at that time were Ahab and Jezebel. The Prophet Elijah, Elisha's mentor, told Elisha to inform a commander in Ahab and Jezebel's Army named Jehu that he would be the next King after he removed Ahab and Jezebel. So, Elisha appointed a young prophet to deliver this special message to Jehu. Jehu accepted the message as from God. Ahab was killed in an unrelated battle and Jehu helped to remove Jezebel and others in support of her, while becoming the next King of Israel – just as the prophets had said.

But remember, Jehu was not a religious or political leader and neither is Donald Trump. So, what's my point? The current political establishment has been seduced and intimidated by a "Jezebel and Ahab" spirit (attitude) while making fear-based decisions in response to the latest whims of "political correctness." Like in Elisha's time, the spirit of Ahab and Jezebel has deceived many into believing lies through gossip and slander, while responding in fear to intimidation and fear of material loss. They feel that they have to follow the current political correctness or they will be ostracized, shamed and defeated. But, like Jehu, Donald Trump is full of faith and determination and armed with a Biblical Worldview - believing that God is with him and with his God all things are possible.

Trump defies the PC Police while honoring Biblical principles and chooses not to allow the PC Police to intimidate him. In other words, Donald Trump lives like Jesus taught – fearlessly from the inside, out. However, the people that are being awakened by Mr. Trump are those that have been living in fear. Like the Pied Piper, Donald Trump has hit a magical chord with the Silent Majority. He has awakened a sleeping giant!

And, like in Elisha's time, there are many people in America today that feel the same way that Donald Trump does, but they have been afraid to speak their convictions. They have sat passively by and not even voted in the last two presidential elections. But, then a leader like Mr. Trump rises up and speaks with passion and conviction while articulating the beliefs of many that have silently criticized the federal government and both political parties. He put gas on the fire of their political passions. And when Donald Trump started talking their language, he awakened and inspired a sleeping giant in America – the Silent Majority, also called "values voters." Their unspoken mantra has been brilliantly articulated by Mr. Trump.

> **Perhaps the name of an old movie can best describe this group:**
>
> **"I'm Mad as Hell and I'm Not Going to Take It Anymore!"**

The Silent Majority has awakened, and Donald Trump has become their spokesperson and commanding officer like Jehu did during the time of the Prophet Elisha! And very soon we will hear the words, "Who is on my side?" Eventually, someone will hear the words, "Throw her down," referring to

Queen Jezebel. But right now, the spirit of Jehu is saying, "What do you know about peace and prosperity? Join me, and I'll show you what real peace and prosperity are!" And that will be the end of the reign of the Republican (Ahab Spirit) and the Democratic (Jezebel Spirit) establishments as we know them today!

The Republican Party Establishment has been personifying the Spirit of Ahab, while the Democratic Party has been personifying the Spirit of Jezebel. Both are about to be pruned by the mighty hand of God in response to the prayers of God's people, according to 2 Chronicles 7:14. And one person that is leading the charge is Donald Trump, seemingly one of the most unlikely people to do God's work.

But God has been using strange men and women to do his work for thousands of years. One great example of that is King David who was the youngest of the house of Jesse and the shepherd of his dad's sheep.

Donald Trump - the US President and Commander in Chief

Like Jehu in 2 Kings, Donald Trump surprised everyone. Hardly anyone believed Mr. Trump could defeat Hillary Clinton and the Democrats. Not even the Republican Party or the huge silent majority thought Trump could win. A record number of the silent majority, largely consisting of self-identified Christians, voted this time, dramatically influencing the outcome of the election. The historical results of this election will be analyzed for many years to attempt to find out how Trump won. However, I believe there's one simple answer – The Jehu Factor!

Once Donald Trump was elected as the next President of the United States, many still stubbornly fought against Trump by spreading unsubstantiated rumors and attempting various state-wide vote recounting efforts. However, in one state's recount effort, Donald Trump actually *gained* votes. In short, the recount effort has been unsuccessful in stopping The Trump Factor, because it's actually The God Factor or the Jehu Factor - if you prefer.

So what does all of this mean? I believe that God has heard our prayers in America and is healing our land. That healing has started with the election of Donald Trump. God is using President Trump to unite the silent majority and many others that will respond to his mantra to "make America great again".

**Like Jehu, President Trump is saying,
"You don't know what peace is!
Follow me! I'll show you what true peace and prosperity are!"**

When many Americans looked at Donald Trump, they saw a rich businessman. But when God looked at Donald Trump, he saw a great leader - a leader that could be used to prune the unfruitful branches of the US Government and awaken the Body of Christ to fulfill her original mandate - to take dominion, be fruitful and multiply (Genesis 1).

When Father-God answers our prayers, he frequently gives us what we need, not what we want. And in the words of a popular TV Show in the 1950's, "Father Knows Best."

Proverbs 3:5-6, "Trust in the Lord with all of your heart and lean not on your understanding. In all your ways acknowledge him and he will direct your paths."

When David's family looked at him, they saw a shepherd boy. But when God looked at David, God saw a king.

Friend, when God looks at you, what does he see?

Bibliography

The Day of the Saints, by Dr. Bill Hamon, Destiny Image Publishers, PO Box 310, Shippensburg, PA 17257

Revelation Commentary Manual, by Irving Baxter, Jr., published by End Time Ministries, PO Box 2066, Richmond, IN 4737-2066, www.endtime.com

Becoming Melchizedek, by Dr. Charles Robinson, Melchizedek International,
www.Melchizedek.International

The Messianic Church Arising, by Dr. Robert Heidler, Robert Heidler Publisher, **ISBN:** 0979167825

Kenneth Copeland, a quote at the Kenneth Copeland Ministries 2016 S.W. Believers Convention in Fort Worth, TX, www.kcm.org.

SPIRIT-LED PUBLISHING

SpiritLedPublishing.com

Select "Tell me how inexpensively and professionally you can publish my book."

In this season of the end-time, it is absolutely critical that the *arrows of intercession that we shoot hit the mark all the time.*

The prophet Jeremiah spoke these words: **"Yes, prepare to attack Babylon, all you nations round about. Let your *archers* shoot at her. *Spare no arrows*, for she has sinned against the Lord."** (Jeremiah 50:14.)

Spirit-Led Publishing is your full-service publishing house. We help publish your Spirit-Led "Master Pieces."

Let your "arrows"—your books—hit their mark. Launch them through Spirit-Led Publishing.

Notes

About the Author

Larry grew up in Grand Prairie, Texas, a suburb of the city of Dallas located in the heart of Dallas and Fort Worth. After graduating from Grand Prairie High School, Larry earned a Bachelor of Science degree from Dallas Baptist University and a Master of Education degree from the University of North Texas in Denton. He has taught for Shady Grove Christian Academy, Cleburne I.S.D., Arlington High School, Grand Prairie High School, Irving High School, Prince Career Institute, Shady Grove Christian Academy, North Lake College, Cenikor Foundation and El Centro College of the Dallas County Community College District. Larry is certified to teach freshman level Bible courses through the Seminary Extension Program of the National Southern Baptist Convention, serving all six of their accredited seminaries in the USA, including Southwestern Baptist Theological Seminary in Fort Worth, Texas.

Larry was first published at the age of 12, after he enter a local newspaper competition, while writing an essay to the Grand Prairie Daily News about his baseball coach. He was awarded first place. After which, Larry and his family as well as his coach and family enjoyed an all-expense paid summer vacation to Hot Springs Arkansas!

As a successful corporate trainer, public high school teacher, adult education manager and college instructor/administrator, Larry has freely shared his lessons-learned in various publications for the last 25 years. While creating and writing an academic "Ask the Bible Column" for a weekly national publication, Larry has also written and produced training materials/manuals for churches, businesses, newspapers, public schools, colleges and universities, while managing budgets and motivating students and employees. UMR Communications, the SBTEXAN, the Dallas Morning News, ChristianPost.Com and the Star Telegram have published Larry's insightful, candid and sometimes poignant articles.

One of Larry's favorite original sayings is,
"If education isn't practical, it's practically no good."

www.ingramcontent.com/pod-product-compliance
Lightning Source LLC
LaVergne TN
LVHW051827080426
835512LV00018B/2752